Itsuwaribito·空·

YUUKI IINUMA

Contents

RUSTLE

WHAT SHALL WE DO. RYUBI?

HOW SHALL WE GET REVENGE ON THE TANUKI?

I DON'T WANT THIS TO BE DIFFICULT, SO...

HMM... I HAVE AN IDEA!

Chapter 118
Trio

SOMETHING IS COMING...
FWOOOOSH
SOMETHING VERY BAD...
LONG AGO...
...THERE WAS AN...INCIDENT... THAT CAUSED THE TANUKI OF THIS VILLAGE TO HATE HUMANS.
PLEASE TELL US WHAT HAPPENED.

I WILL...
ELDER!

FWSH
TSUKU-MO?

CRA
CKLE

WHAT IS IT, TSUKUMO? YOU'RE UPSET.
ELDER!
IT'S THEM!

THE ONES...
...WHO DESTROYED OUR VILLAGE ONCE BEFORE!

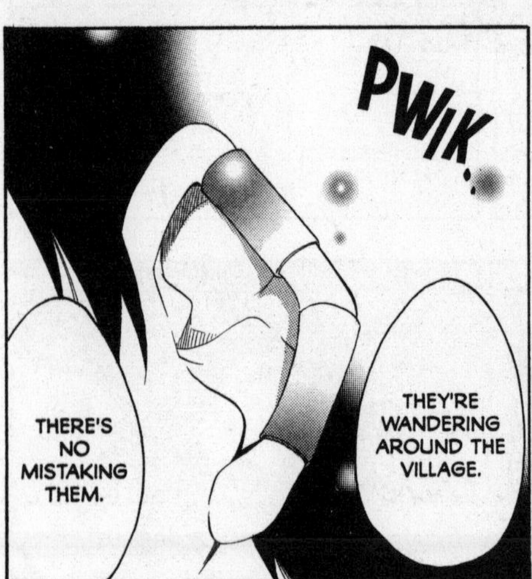

*ONE RI = APPROX. FOUR KILOMETERS

WHERE ARE YOU GOING? DO YOU MEAN TO FIGHT ALONE?
THAT IS RECKLESS.

THIS DOESN'T SOUND GOOD! WHAT SHOULD WE DO?
ALL WE KNOW IS THAT THERE ARE ENEMIES ABOUT.

YEAH, SO DON'T GET ANY IDEAS.
!
THERE'S NOTHING YOU CAN DO.
HMPH!

WE WON'T KNOW UNTIL WE TRY!
BOO
Boo!

ONE OF THE ENEMY HAS THE SAME POWERS I HAVE.
KNOWING THAT, DO YOU STILL WANT TO FIGHT?

!
THE SAME POWERS?
ON YOUR KNEES, UZUME!
THAT DOES PRESENT PROBLEMS...

I SEE THAT COOLED YOU OFF. SO STAY OUT OF THIS...
...AND LEAVE, NOW!

SH
OO
?!
A PILLAR OF FLAME ?!
OH NO...
I'M TOO LATE!

BWO
Heh heh...
Heh heh...
WOW!
LOOK AT IT BURN!
FWOOOSH
THE VILLAGE...
MY PEOPLE...
ALL GONE...
WE COULD NOT EVEN EVACUATE...
SHUMP
NIBYO AND IWASHI AND MINAMO WERE STILL IN THE VILLAGE!
NO...
TMP
TMP

IT'S ALL RIGHT, WE'RE OKAY.
EVERYONE'S OKAY, HUMAN AND TANUKI.

!
MINAMO!

WAP
I'M SO GLAD TO SEE YOU!
MMF!
I WAS ABLE TO FORE-SEE THIS CLEARLY ENOUGH TO...

EVACUATE THEM?!
AND NO ONE WAS HURT?!
NOT SERIOUSLY, THOUGH...
...AT FIRST THEY DIDN'T BELIEVE ME.
PLEASE BELIEVE ME! YOU MUST RUN!
...
PSST PSST
Can it be true?
It can't be!
She must be lying.

LEAVE THIS TO ME!
I'LL COPY UTSUHO.
AFTER ALL, I'M AN ITSUWARIBITO TOO.
I'LL TELL A GOOD LIE!
WHAT'LL YOU DO, KITTY-BOY?
KSHING
VEEN
GAH
GAH
GAAAH
WHAM
TROMP
THIS WAY! HURRY!
YIKES
I, NIBYO, AM A KILLER OF TANUKI!
I PUT 'EM IN A STEW AND EAT 'EM!
Graaaah!
KYAA
AAH!
THAT'S HOW HE DID IT.
NIBYO DID WELL. GOOD FOR HIM!

COME THIS WAY.
I'LL TAKE YOU TO THE OTHERS.
OH, THANK YOU.

LET'S GO!
Take my hand, Grandfather!

...

C'MON, TSUKU-MO...
YOU MUST BE WORRIED ABOUT THEM.

BY THE WAY, YOU SAID WE COULDN'T DO ANYTHING...
...BUT, AS YOU SEE, HUMANS CAN BE SURPRISING. YOU SHOULD HAVE A LITTLE MORE FAITH.

...
LEAVE ME ALONE.
GRR...

SWF

SHHH

SP S S

ELDER!

YOU'RE SAFE!

I AM GLAD YOU ARE ALL WELL.

WE OWE IT TO THE HUMANS.

UTSUHO-SAMA! YOU'RE SAFE!

HIKAE, I HEARD ABOUT WHAT YOU DID.

WELL, YEAH...

I DID MY BEST, IS ALL.

YOU SEEM A BIT... DARK THOUGH.

YOU KNOW HOW IT IS, EVERY LIE COMES WITH A COST...

?

UM...

...?

PA
POOF
POOF

THANK YOU FOR HELPING US!
WHOA!

WE MISJUDGED YOU. IT SEEMS SOME HUMANS ARE GOOD.
WE HOPE YOU CAN FORGIVE US.
OH, THERE'S NOTHING TO FOR-GIVE!

I'M SURE FROM NOW ON WE CAN ALL GET ALONG.
THANKS TO MINAMO AND HIKAE.
I'm so happy...
PEEK
FLINCH

TA
TMP
?
THEY DO THAT WHEN-EVER THEY SEE ME NOW.

I SAID I'D PUT 'EM IN A STEW AND EAT 'EM UP.
THEY KNOW I WAS LYING...
...BUT THEY'RE STILL SCARED.
They won't come near me.

BUT IT'S NOT LIKE I CARE.
STILL, NIBYO... GOOD JOB!

I shoulda told a different lie...

PAT

!

NIBYO-SAN NOT SCARY!
YOU SAVE US! THANK YOU!

...
POCHI ...

I'M HAPPY AS LONG AS YOU ARE!

I KNOW WHAT YOU'RE GOING TO SAY, ELDER, BUT THE ENEMY WILL SOON FIND US. I MUST FINISH THIS.

YOU CANNOT DO IT ALONE, TSUKUMO.

THEY HAVE GREATER STRENGTH.

BESIDES, TWO OF THEM WERE FROM THIS VILLAGE. FIGHTING THEM WOULD BE-
!

AND THAT'S WHY...

...I HAVE TO DO THIS MYSELF.

NO!

HWIP

TSU-KU-MO!

...

GRAND-FATHER...

WHAT CAN YOU TELL ME ABOUT TSUKUMO'S POWER?

IT COULD HELP.

HMM...

I'M SORRY, BUT I REALLY DON'T KNOW VERY MUCH ABOUT IT.

TSUKUMO ALONE AMONG ALL THE VILLAGERS CAN WIELD THAT POWER.

I WAS WONDERING ABOUT THAT. SO IT'S NOT SOMETHING ALL TANUKI CAN DO?

HEY!

WHAT'S BEEN GOING ON?

THE VILLAGE IS ON FIRE.

THE KID WHO CAME FOR US SAID SOMETHING ABOUT EVACU-ATING.

CHOZA...

SO YOU'RE ALL RIGHT.

HOW IS UZUME?

TELL ME WHAT HAPPENED.

I SEE...

FOR SOME REASON HE NEEDS TO KNOW HIS OPPONENT'S NAME TO USE HIS POWER.

THAT MAY BE USE-FUL.

I GUESS SO.

I'D SAY IT'S FOR ***SURE***.

ALSO...

HOW CAN YOU MOVE BUT UZUME CAN'T?

CAN'T HELP YOU THERE. I...

AH! !

LAST NAMES!

UZUME HAS NO LAST NAME, RIGHT?
DO YOU MIND IF I GIVE YOU ONE?
HOW'S UZUME SOUND?
YOU DO THOUGH. IT'S HABAKI. BUT TSUKUMO DOESN'T KNOW THAT.
HE'D NEED TO IN ORDER TO TAKE YOU OUT WITH HIS POWER.
AND THAT'S HOW WE COUNTER IT!
EVEN IF SOMEONE USES THAT POWER AGAIN...
SO WE KEEP OUR FULL NAMES A SECRET!
THAT DOESN'T SOUND TOO HARD!
TSUKUMO TOLD US TO LEAVE BECAUSE WE'RE OUT-SIDERS...
...BUT SINCE TWO OF THE ENEMY ARE FROM THIS VILLAGE...
...THEY KNOW HIS NAME, AND HE KNOWS THEY KNOW IT.
FWIP
CLOMP
THE IDIOT'S GOT PRIDE...
...BUT IT'LL LEAD TO HIS DOWNFALL UNLESS WE OUTSIDERS TAKE ACTION!

Chapter 119 Cursed Power

FWOO
OOOSH

?!
HOW ODD...

GRAH!
TOMP
!
I WONDERED WHAT ALL THAT NOISE WAS...
IT'S YOU, TSUKUMO.
LONG TIME NO SEE.
VEEEEN
AND NOW, GOODBYE.
SAVE US ALL SOME TROUBLE AND DIE, OKAY?
...
WHY YOU...

Chapter 119
Cursed Power

HOW COULD YOU DO THIS...
...TO THE VILLAGE?! IT'S YOUR BIRTHPLACE!

DECADES AGO YOU JOINED UP WITH A HUMAN AND KILLED YOUR PEOPLE!
NOW YOU'RE BACK! WHY?!
...
OH, MY DEAR TSUKUMO... I THINK YOU KNOW!
REVENGE!
WHAT I HAD TO ENDURE HERE CAN NEVER BE FORGIVEN, SO I MEAN TO FINISH YOU ALL OFF FOR GOOD AND ALL!

ESPECIALLY *YOU*, TSUKUMO.
YOU MUST PAY FOR WHAT YOU DID TO RYUBI.
!
HAS HE RETURNED AS WELL?
I WON'T TELL YOU.
YOU'RE AS GOOD AS DEAD, ANYWAY.
OR HAVE YOU FORGOTTEN THAT I POSSESS THE SAME POWER AS YOU?

WITH MY OPPONENT'S NAME, I CAN MAKE HIM OR HER OBEY ANY COMMAND.
IT IS THE *CURSED POWER*...
...THAT ONLY YOU AND I HAVE.

...

WHAT SHALL I COMMAND YOU TO DO?
KNEEL? CRY? APOLOGIZE?
GROVELING WOULD BE NICE...

I KNOW!

TSUKUMO MUJINA! IMPALE YOURSELF THROUGH THE CHEST!
MAMI TSUZUMI! CLOSE YOUR MOUTH FOREVER!

HWIP
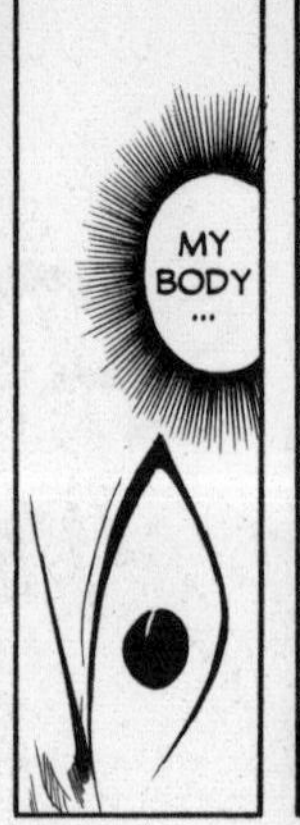
MY BODY ...

GRB
SNAP
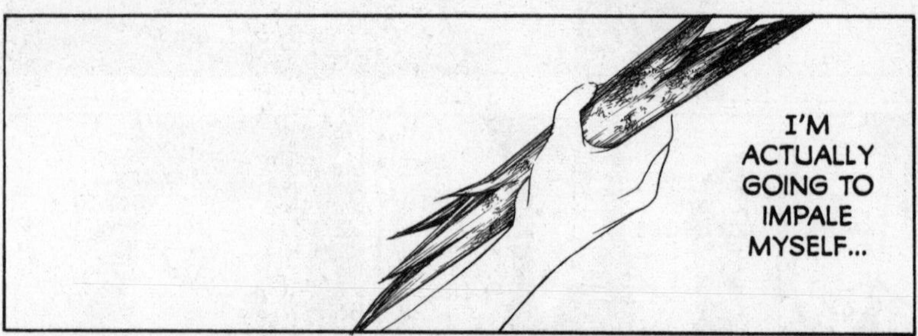
I'M ACTUALLY GOING TO IMPALE MYSELF...
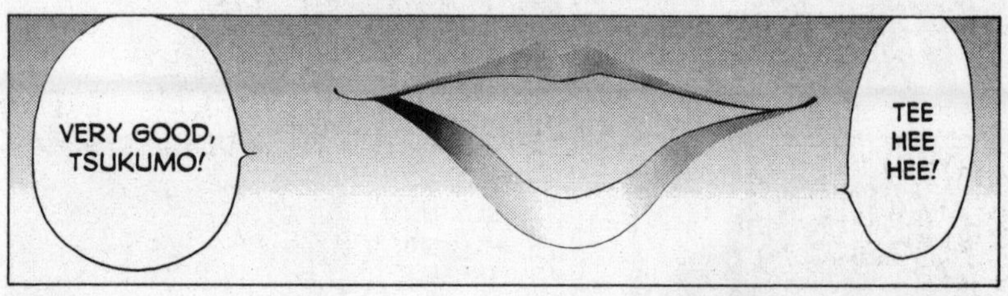
TEE HEE HEE!
VERY GOOD, TSUKUMO!
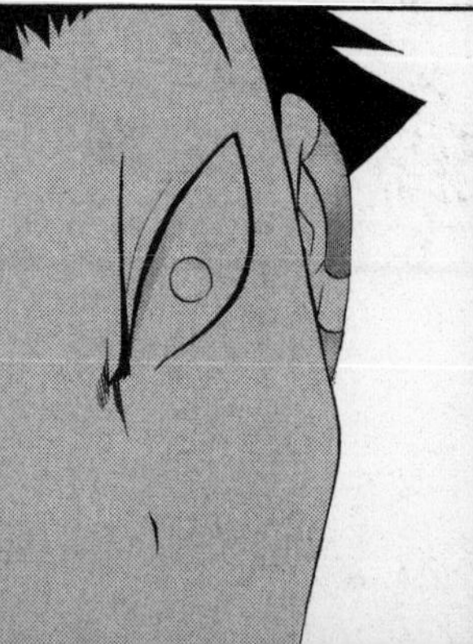

?!
I SAY! WHY SO SUR-PRISED?

AFTER ALL THIS TIME...
MY COMMAND DIDN'T WORK!
...DID YOU THINK WE WOULDN'T HAVE FIGURED OUT A WAY TO COUNTER YOUR POWER?
AS I'M SURE YOU KNOW...
...THE CURSED POWER IS NOT UN-BEATABLE.
GWIP
OH WELL... GOODBYE, TSUKUMO.
STAB

?!
OW...
YOU...
THAT... HURTS!
WELL, YEAH, YOU IDIOT! HEY...
WHO ARE YOU?!
CLOMP

JUST SOME...

...ITSU-WARIBITO PASSING THROUGH.

TA TMP

ITSU-WARIBI-TO...

THE HUMANS IN THE VILLAGE...

THREE AREN'T HERE...

Ugh... this sucks...

I'M GLAD YOU'RE ALL RIGHT.

UTSUHO TALKS ROUGH...
...BUT HE CAME TO HELP.

...
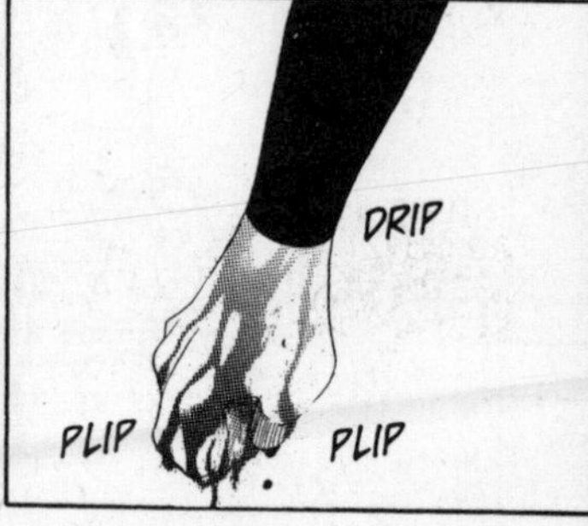
DRIP
PLIP
PLIP

STAY OUT OF THIS, YOU... WHOEVER YOU ARE!
OR I'LL SEND YOU ALL INTO THE NEXT WORLD!

YOU'RE MORE THAN WEL-COME TO TRY!
BUT WE'RE ONTO YOU!
YOU NEED YOUR OPPONENTS' LAST NAMES, IF THEY HAVE THEM!
UZUME'S THE ONLY ONE OF US WHO DOESN'T, SO THAT'S THAT!

...
SIGH...

I'M NOT STUPID, YOU KNOW.
WE RECONNOI-TERED THE SITUATION BEFORE SHOWING OURSELVES.
WE KNEW YOU WERE IN THE VILLAGE.
DID YOU THINK I WAS REALLY SURPRISED WHEN YOU SHOWED UP HERE?

AND BY THE WAY...
...THAT THING ABOUT NOT KNOWING YOUR FULL NAMES...
SHF

I'M AFRAID THAT'S NOT EXACTLY TRUE.
SWIP
IT CAN BE PRETTY HARD TO KEEP THINGS LIKE THAT SECRET WHEN YOU DON'T YET KNOW...
...THAT THEY SHOULD BE.

?!
WHAT'S THAT?

HM...
I'VE SEEN THAT BOOK...
!
GAH! LOOK AT THAT!

IT'S GOT OUR NAMES IN IT!

Utsuho Azako
Pochi
Neya Muito
Koshiro Yakuma

Hikae Nibyo
Iwashi Yashima
Minamo Kawazu
Uzume
Choza Habaki

YIKES!

THAT'S THE INN GUEST REGISTRY I WROTE IN!

NEYA...

I DIDN'T KNOW!

YOU SAW THAT SHRIMP USE HIS POWER ON UZUME.

DIDN'T YOU EVER THINK ABOUT BEING MORE CAREFUL...

...WITH YOUR NAMES?

...

HEE HEE HEE!
THOUGHT YOU HAD ME, DIDN'T YOU.!
OH NO...
IT'S ALL MY FAULT...
OH, WE HAVE YOU, ALL RIGHT.
IF YOU THINK THAT BOOK EXPOSES US TO YOUR POWER...
...YOU'RE IN FOR A BIG DISAPPOINT-MENT.
?!
WHAT'S HE MEAN?
IS HE BLUFF-ING?
HE'S RIGHT, MAMI. THAT BOOK WON'T HELP YOU.
!
RYUBI!

?!
IT'S HIM...
RYUBI!
GREETINGS, EVERYONE.
IT'S BEEN A WHILE, TSUKU-MO.

SO THAT'S THEIR LEADER...
!

WHY YOU–

NOW, NOW...
AFTER ALL THIS TIME, YOU STILL HATE ME?
UNDER-STAND-ABLE.

DECADES AGO, THESE TWO BETRAYED THE VILLAGE...
...AND DESTROYED IT.
IT'S ALL MY FAULT YOUR PARENTS DIED.

!

HIS PARENTS ...?
URGH

BUT RYUBI...

...YOU TOO HAVE SUFFERED BECAUSE OF THE CURSE HE PLACED ON YOU.

AS THANKS ...
...LET'S KILL 'EM ALL NOW!

!
CLOMP

BRING IT ON THEN.
AT THIS POINT, WE CAN STILL WIN.
THE WORST THING WOULD BE FOR THEM TO RUN.

NO, NO...
YOU HEARD WHAT HE SAID.
WE HAVE THAT INN REGISTRY, BUT IT'S MORE OF A DANGER TO US THAN TO THEM.

HOW SO?
THE NAMES WRITTEN THERE...
ARE THEY ACTUALLY AS EASY TO READ AS YOU SEEM TO THINK?

IS THAT SORA AJAKO?
NEYA ROKUTO? KOSHIRO YAKUMA? HIKAE NINEKO?
NO, I DON'T THINK SO...
IF YOU DON'T READ THE NAMES CORRECTLY, YOUR POWER COULD BACKFIRE.

HE NOTICED. AND WHAT'S MORE...
MY NAME WAS RIGHT...
BABMP BABMP

ON TOP OF THAT, YOU DON'T KNOW WHO HAS WHICH NAME.
IT WOULD, AS YOU KNOW, BE VERY FOOLISH TO GUESS.
THEY ALSO OUTNUMBER US.

BESIDES, I'M WEAK AND COULD HARDLY RUN, MUCH LESS FIGHT.
IF YOU HAD TO PROTECT ME, WHAT CHANCE WOULD WE HAVE?
!
HE SAYS HE'S WEAK?
HE'S BLATHERING, REVEALING ALL THEIR WEAKNESSES...
IS HE LYING?
THIS ENCOUNTER HOLDS TOO MANY RISKS WE DON'T NEED TO TAKE.
GOOD-BYE.
FOR NOW.
UH-OH! IF THEY GET AWAY AND REGROUP, WE'RE COOKED!
STOP THEM!
DON'T LET THEM GET AWAY!
IT'S NOW OR NEVER!
WHSH

Chapter 120 Lilly

THAT ONE WASN'T FOOLED.
HE KNOWS IT WOULD BE FATAL TO LET US GO. WE COULD HAVE A PROBLEM WITH HIM.

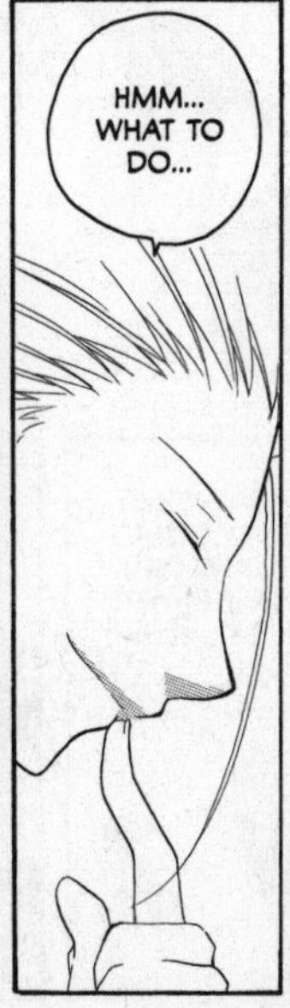
HMM... WHAT TO DO...

ALL RIGHT, LET'S SPLIT UP AND RUN.
WHSH

OH, GREAT ...
EVERYBODY PICK ONE AND CHASE 'EM!
WHSH

I'M GOING LEFT...
GRB

Chapter 120
Lilly

TMP TMP TMP
TMP TMP
TSK!
HE'S VERY PERSIS-TENT!
STOP CHASING ME!
LET'S SEE... A BOY'S NAME...
SORA AJAKO! STAND STILL!
TMP
Hmph
WRONG...
IS THIS... NINEKO? JIBYO?
HIKAE JINEKO! STOP RIGHT THERE!
POCHI! HARM YOURSELF!
KARASU-ZUME! DON'T MOVE!
CHOSA HABAKARIKI! CROUCH DOWN!
TMP TMP
...!

RATS!
NOTHING'S WORKING!
WHAT'S WITH THESE WEIRD NAMES ANYWAY?

FINE, I'LL DO WHAT RYUBI SAID...
...AND RUN.
FWSH

ARGH!
I GET IT... SHE...

TUG
GRB
!

TATATATATUMPTMP
GYAAAAH!

UGH...

THUD

HEH! CAUGHT YOU.

YOUR PHYSICAL ABILITIES AREN'T SO GREAT.

WHAT'S THE MATTER, LILLY?

UM... I THOUGHT I HEARD MAMI'S VOICE.

TP

TP

I HOPE SHE'S ALL RIGHT.

DON'T WORRY, SHE'LL BE FINE.

OUR PHYSICAL ABILITIES AREN'T IMPRESSIVE...

...BUT FROM WHAT I'VE SEEN...

WHSH

OH...

YOU CAUGHT UP.

NO, NO, MY BODY REALLY IS WEAK. WISH IT WAS OTHERWISE.

IF I TRIED HIDING IT, YOU'D FIND OUT SOON ENOUGH.

THAT'S WHY I TOLD YOU.

BUT, Y'SEE, IT DOESN'T REALLY MATTER.

TUMP

!

SWSH

RYUBI CAN'T FIGHT YOU, BUT I WILL.

!
OKAY, SHE COULD BE SERIOUS TROUBLE...

SWIP

WIGGLE WIGGLE WIGGLE WIGGLE
WIGGLE WIGGLE WIGGLE

?
WIGGLE WIGGLE WIGGLE WIGGLE WIGGLE
?!
WIGGLE WIGGLE WIGGLE WIGGLE WIGGLE WIGGLE

WIGGLE

PA WOOF
?!
!
SH...SHE TURNED INTO *ME*!
SWIF

YANK

M-MY BODY'S MOVING ALL ON ITS OWN!

GRB
!!

SO SHE CAN TAKE SOME-ONE'S FORM...
...AND *CONTROL* THEM!

WH
UD

UTSU-HO!
WHAT SHOULD I DO?
SHOULD I BEAT THAT GIRL UP?

THAT...
TMP
...MIGHT NOT BE A GOOD IDEA.

PINCH

OW!
PANG

HIKAE! DON'T MOVE! IF YOU ATTACK HER, YOU'LL HURT NEYA, THE PERSON SHE'S COPYING!
AND SHE COULD USE HER ABILITY TO KILL YOU!

?!
EVEN THOUGH I CAN'T DIE?

ALL RIGHT, LILLY, SHALL WE FINISH THEM OFF?
...
SWIP

SHANNG

SHING

HWIP

EESH...
IF I FIGHT BACK, I'LL HURT NEYA.
BUT IF I RUN, NEYA WILL STILL BE UNDER HER CONTROL!

WHICH MEANS...

N-NOOOO!
STOP!

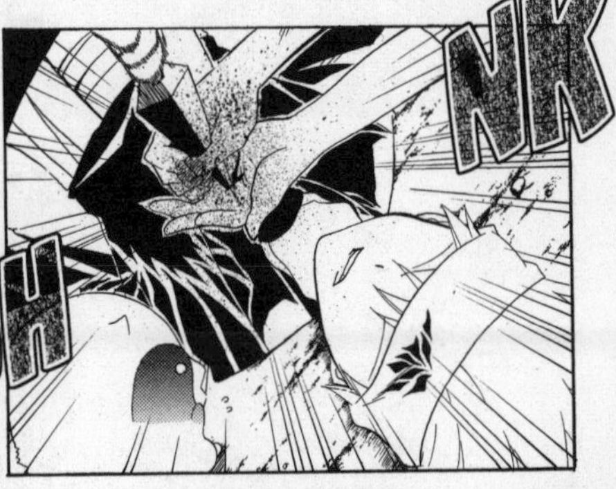
NK
SH

HEY! WHAT'RE YOU-

NEYA MUITO. SLEEP.
PSST
GASP
!
SHMP
I HEARD HER NAME FROM KOSHIRO.
LILLY CAN'T CONTROL SOMEONE WHO ISN'T CONSCIOUS.

NO. I'LL LET YOU LEAVE.

A GIRL? HA! YOU'RE A TANUKI WHO'S TAKEN THAT FORM.

I DON'T KNOW *WHAT* SEX YOU ARE.

I SHOULD JUST KILL YOU, BUT THAT'S NOT AS SIMPLE AS IT USED TO BE.

SO I'LL TAKE YOU PRISONER.

!

DON'T THINK I LIKE IT.

LET ME GO, YOU FOOL!

I CAN'T LET YOU CAPTURE ME!

!

HEY! HOLD STILL!

GET OFF ME, YOU–

FWISH

!

SHUMP
OH NO!
?!

URGH ...
TRMBL
TRMBL
!

HA!
HMM...
I WAS WONDERING WHY YOU HID YOUR FACE.

I DON'T NEED MY POWER TO IMMOBILIZE YOU.
YOU'RE NOT WORTH THE TROUBLE.
FWIP
FWIP
...

AND I WON'T KILL YOU.
A GUY WHO STOPS MOVING IN A FIGHT IS JUST BAGGAGE.

I'LL LEAVE YOU TO SLOW UP YOUR COMPANIONS!
...!

YOUR POWER...

THOSE ENEMIES...

TELL ME...

WHAT IS ALL THIS ABOUT?

Chapter 121 The Village's Past

TELL ME...
WHAT HAS SET TANUKI AGAINST TANUKI?

...
NO.

!
IT'S NONE OF YOUR AFFAIR.

TSK...
HE STILL WON'T OPEN UP...

I'D LIKE TO KNOW, TSUKUMO.

TUMP
HEY, DOC...

YOU'RE LATE.
RIGHT...
Because I...
...got stabbed...

TSUKU-MO...

YOU SAY IT'S...

...NOT OUR AFFAIR, YET YOU HELPED UTSUHO AND THE OTHERS.

WE ARE IN YOUR DEBT.

WHAT HAPPENS TO YOU NOW CONCERNS US.

I KNOW YOU HATE HUMANS...
...AND I'M NOT SURE HOW MUCH WE CAN HELP.

BUT WILL YOU TRUST US...
...AND GIVE US SOME IDEA OF WHAT'S GOING ON?

FINE.
CHITCHORIINA...
...I HAVE TO TELL YOU SOME-THING.

LET'S GO BACK TO THE VILLAGE.

Chapter 121
The Village's Past

!
CLOMP

CHOZA!

...!
STAGGER
ARE YOU ALL RIGHT?!

ARE YOU INJURED?
YOU'RE ALONE, SO I GUESS THE GIRL GOT AWAY.
DOESN'T LOOK LIKE YOU DID MUCH BETTER.

URGH! BECAUSE OF THIS TATTOO, I LOOK INCOMPETENT...
GRND

HEY, PIP-SQUEAK. FIX UZUME, WOULD YA?
HE COULD'VE MADE A DIFFERENCE.

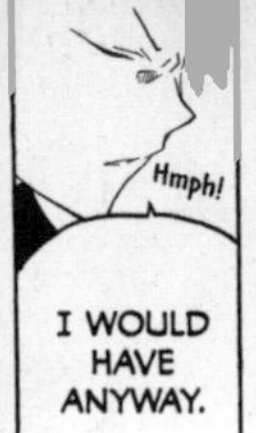

Hmph!
I WOULD HAVE ANYWAY.

ARR!
...

...
AW MAN... SO MUCH FRICTION IN THE AIR!

UTSUHO, WHAT DID YOU MEAN ABOUT THAT CURVY BABE BEING ABLE TO KILL ME?

UM... WELL, I THINK SHE CAN.

I'LL TALK TO TSUKUMO AND TELL YOU WHEN I'M SURE.

HMM...

SPSSSH

TSUKUMO! CHIT-CHORIINA! YOU'RE SAFE!

GLOOM
YEAH, BUT...
URGH URGH
...IT DIDN'T GO VERY WELL.

C'MON. HURRY UP AND FIX UZUME.

FWIP
UZUME! ARE YOU ALL RIGHT?

YES...
RUB
RUB

DOES THAT HURT, UZUME?
RUB
RUB
I'M JUST *FINE*...

I'll bet he is...

OH!
HEY, YOU'RE ALL BACK!
HOW'D IT GO? DIDJA BEAT 'EM?

STOMP STOMP STOMP
STRRRETCH
OW!

WHAT'S THE BIG IDEA?!
THAT'S WHAT I'D LIKE TO ASK!
TO THINK OF WHAT WE WENT THROUGH WHILE YOU WERE JUST LOLLING AROUND...

BUT I CAN'T MOVE!
STAYING IN THE SAME POSITION IS PAINFUL...
SO YOU NEED A LAP TO REST YOUR HEAD IN?
IT'S NICE. YOU SHOULD TRY IT.

HMPH!

CHOZA...
UZUME. MOVE FREELY.
TWITCH
EH?

WOW! I CAN MOVE!
HWIP
...

TAP

SO I'M OKAY...
...BUT HOW ARE YOU?

IT'S YOUR TATTOO, ISN'T IT.

...
YEAH, I GUESS.

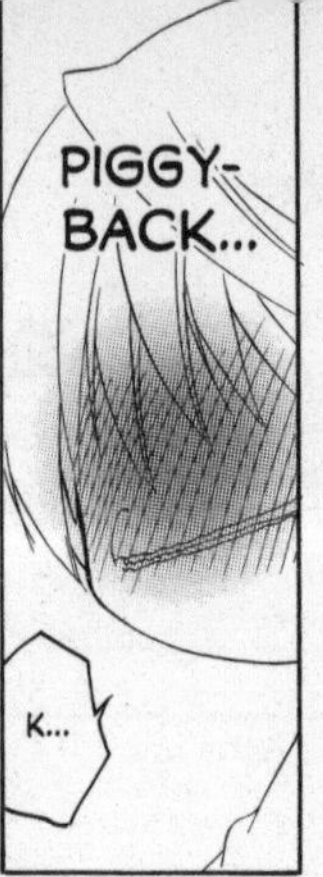

ALL RIGHT, CHIT-CHORII-NA...

HOW OLD ARE YOU NOW?

WE MET WHEN POCHI WAS EIGHT MONTHS OLD.

WE TRAVELED A WHILE, SO POCHI'S NOW OVER ONE YEAR OLD.

Hm?
Hmm?
Hmmm?

IN THAT CASE...

...POCHI'S POWER SHOULD ALREADY BE AVAILABLE.

ONE-YEAR-OLD TANUKIS CAN TRANSFORM. ONCE THEY DO, THEY'RE GROWN-UPS.

OHHH...
THERE ARE MANY WAYS TO TRANS-FORM.
YOU MUST FIND YOUR OWN WAY, CHITCHORIINA.
BUT BEFORE WE TALK ABOUT THE PAST, THERE ARE OTHER MATTERS TO DISCUSS.
AND AS YOUR BETROTHED, I MUST MAKE AN ADMISSION TO YOU.
Hm?
I...
...CANNOT RETURN TO MY TANUKI FORM.
AND I CAN'T TAKE ANOTHER FORM. I'M LIKE THIS FOR LIFE.
?!
AS THE PRICE OF MY WORD POWER, I LIE...
...UNDER A CURSE.

WHAT DO YOU MEAN?

AS LONG AS THEY SATISFY THE CONDITIONS, TANUKI CAN TRANSFORM INTO ANYTHING.
HOWEVER, SOME ACTS ARE FOR-BIDDEN.

THEY INCLUDE GRAVE SINS LIKE KILLING ANOTHER TANUKI.
IF YOU TAKE A CERTAIN FORM AND KILL A TANUKI...
...A CURSE FROM THE VICTIM FALLS UPON YOU...
...AND YOU STAY IN THAT FORM FOR LIFE.

KILL A TANUKI?!
IS HE SAYING...
...HE DID THAT?!

AND WE DO NOT LOOK FAVORABLY UPON KEEPING COMPANY WITH HUMANS...
...BECAUSE OF A... CERTAIN EVENT.

USUALLY, TANUKI CAN ONLY TRANS-FORM...
...BUT LILLY CAN ALSO CONTROL WHOMEVER SHE COPIES...
...BECAUSE SHE WAS BORN TO A HUMAN AND A TANUKI.

!

BECAUSE OF HER UNUSUAL POWER...
...THE TANUKI OF THE VILLAGE WERE AFRAID.
SHE WASN'T MISTREAT-ED...
...BUT SHE FELT ALIENATED ALMOST FROM THE DAY SHE WAS BORN.
SHF

HUMANS AND TANUKI ARE JUST NOT A GOOD MIX.

...
ENOUGH ABOUT THAT. NOW I'LL TELL YOU ABOUT THE EVENT. IT WAS DECADES AGO...

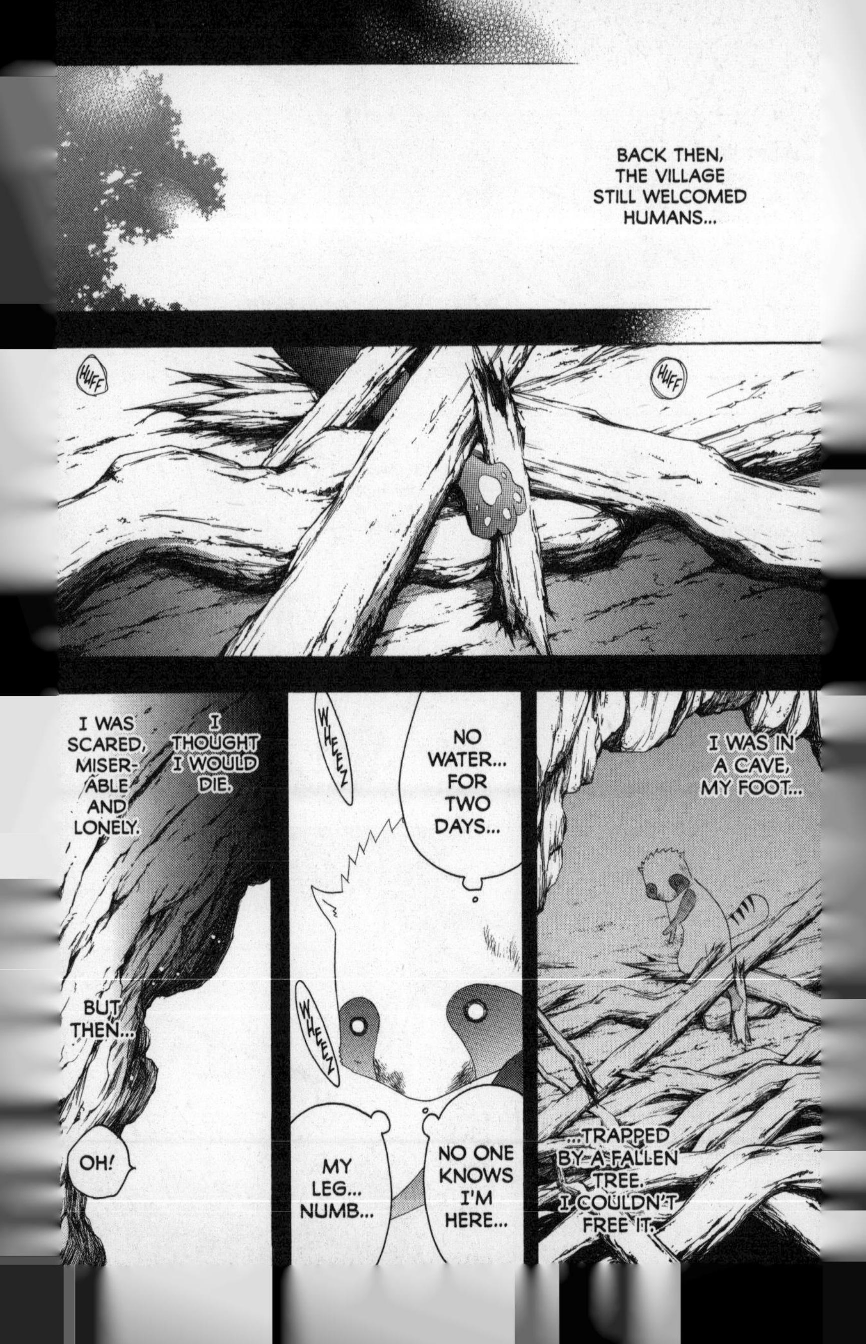
BACK THEN, THE VILLAGE STILL WELCOMED HUMANS...
HUFF
HUFF
I WAS IN A CAVE, MY FOOT...
...TRAPPED BY A FALLEN TREE. I COULDN'T FREE IT.
WHEEZE
NO WATER... FOR TWO DAYS...
WHEEZE
NO ONE KNOWS I'M HERE...
MY LEG... NUMB...
I THOUGHT I WOULD DIE.
I WAS SCARED, MISER-ABLE AND LONELY.
BUT THEN...
OH!

I KNEW IT!
SOME-THING'S THERE!
...A BOY APPEARED.
I HEARD A VOICE.
IT'S OKAY. I'LL HELP YOU.
A HUMAN?
WHEEZ
A... VOICE ...?
WHEEZ
YEAH. I WAS BORN WITH REALLY SHARP HEARING.
DIDN'T EXPECT TO HEAR A TANUKI TALKING THOUGH.
PWIK
HE HAD MYSTERIOUS ORNAMENTS ON HIS EARS.
I'LL GET YOU OUT IN NO TIME.
KTNK...
THERE! THAT SHOULD DO IT!
HE SMILED A LOT...

...AND SAID HIS NAME WAS TSUBAME AKEISHI.
YOU OKAY?
IS IT *HIS* FORM YOU'RE WEAR-ING?
YES.
AFTER-WARDS, I TOOK HIM TO THE VILLAGE.
EVERYONE WELCOMED HIM WARMLY.
TSUBAME SAID HE CAME IN SEARCH OF TREASURE.
Yippee!
Thank you!
Thank you!
We'll prepare a feast!
Take your ease here!

TREAS-URE?
YEAH! IT'S AWESOME! AFTER YOU COLLECT NINE, YOU GET THE TREASURE OF GOD!
A TREASURE SO GREAT THAT WITH IT YOU CAN CHANGE THE WORLD!
I'VE HAD SOME HARD TIMES, SO I...
...WENT TRAVELING TO GATHER THE TREASURE AND IMPROVE MY LIFE!
I LIKE THIS VILLAGE.
IT'S PEACE-FUL AND QUIET.
Yaay!
Yaah!
Yippee!
IT HAS A GENTLE ATMO-SPHERE.
POOF
I GUESS THERE ARE SOME PLACES IN THE WORLD THAT ARE REALLY GREAT.
ARE YOU GOING TO SPEND YOUR LIFE HERE?

PROBABLY. I'M NOW BETROTHED...
Promised to the elder's grandchild...
BE-?!
YOU'RE BETROTHED?! AND TO THE ELDER'S GRANDCHILD?
WHILE I DON'T EVEN HAVE A GIRLFRIEND!
ARE YOU MARRYING FOR MONEY?
ARE YOU A BOY OR A GIRL?
!!
DON'T ASK THAT!
DAYS WERE PEACEFUL IN THE VILLAGE...
...BUT THAT WAS ABOUT TO CHANGE...
HUNH...
I DIDN'T EXPECT...
...BECAUSE OF A CERTAIN MAN.
...TO FIND A VILLAGE HERE.

THE VILLAGE IS NOISIER THESE DAYS.
YEAH...
THAT HUMAN WHO RESCUED TSUKUMO IS HERE.
THE SHORT ONE WITH SPIKY HAIR.
HMM ...
SHALL WE GO BACK TO THE VILLAGE, LILLY?
...
DON'T YOU LIKE IT THERE?
...
RUSTLE
SHOMMP
!
Whoa!
LOOK, LILLY! A HUMAN!
IS HE A TRAV-ELER?

HELLO THERE, YOUNG LADIES!

CAN YOU TELL ME WHERE I AM?

Chapter 122
Pup

A FEW MONTHS AFTER TSUBAME CAME...
GRAH!
A HUMAN AND A PUP...
...ARE EATING MY SNACKS!
I DIDN'T KNOW! WHAT SHOULD WE DO, TSUBAME? DAD'S REALLY MAD!
HERE'S AN IDEA...
YOU APOLOGIZE!
TRIP
!

HMPH!
CALM DOWN.
IT'S NO BIG DEAL.
My snacks...
WHY YOU-!
I'VE NEVER SEEN TSUKUMO HAVING SO MUCH FUN.
HMPH!
WHY'D YOU TRIP ME LIKE THAT? IT'S DANGEROUS!
YEAH, YEAH... I'M SORRY.
YOU TOOK A FALL FOR THE GUY WHO SAVED YOUR LIFE! DON'T GET SO MAD!
THAT WAS MONTHS AGO! HOW LONG ARE YOU GOING TO TALK ABOUT IT?!
URRRGH
AN ADULT BEARS HIS RESPONSI-BILITIES!
THAT'S WHY YOU'RE JUST A PUP.
!
Tsk...
Tsk...

DON'T CALL ME A PUP.
I DON'T LIKE IT...
REALLY? SAY, WHY HAVEN'T YOU MATURED YET?
Like coming of age?
...
ONE YEAR AFTER BIRTH, TANUKI CAN USE THEIR POWER TO TRANSFORM.
ONCE THEY DO, THEY'RE GROWN UP.
BUT THERE ARE DIFFERENT WAYS OF TRANS-FORMING.
SOME TRANS-FORM BY TOUCHING SOMEONE...
POOF
...WHILE OTHERS PLACE A LEAF ON THEIR HEAD.
POOF
BUT I...
YEAH?

I TAKE THE OTHER PERSON'S...

...SOUL.

BY SOUL, YOU MEAN THEIR LIFE?

YES.

AND IF I DO THAT, THEN THEY...

...

OH, I GET IT.

WHEEZ...
WHEEZ...
BEING A PUP IS THE WORST THING FOR A TANUKI.
I'M WRETCHED, PITIFUL AND PATHETIC...
I'M EVEN SICK OF *MYSELF*...
I'LL BE LIKE THIS MY WHOLE LIFE...
SOB...
SNIF
...
HEY, TSUKU-MO?
I'VE BEEN THINKING ABOUT LEAVING THE VILLAGE.
!

HUH? WHY?!
YOU SAID IT'S A GOOD PLACE SO YOU WOULD STAY FOREVER!
YEAH...
IT IS A GOOD PLACE...
...BUT MY PRESENCE...
...MAKES THE OTHER TANUKI UNEASY.
BA BMP
BA BMP
BA BMP
THAT BOTHERS ME.
...
THAT'S ...
...BECAUSE OF LILLY.
SHE WAS BORN OF A TANUKI AND A HUMAN.
SHE HAS A STRANGE POWER.
SHE HASN'T CAUSED ANY PROBLEMS...
...BUT I UNDERSTAND WHY THE VILLAGERS ARE UNEASY.
BESIDES...
...IT'S BEST NOT TO STAND STILL.
LIKE I SAID, I'VE BEEN THROUGH A LOT.
AND I GOT TIRED.

I GREW UNHAPPY WITH THE WORLD...
...AND WENT ON A JOURNEY SEARCHING FOR TREASURE.
I LEARNED SOMETHING HERE.
THERE IS MUCH IN THE WORLD THAT I DON'T KNOW.
THERE'S ALL SORTS OF HAP-PINESS.
I WAS STUCK IN A SMALL WORLD THAT LEFT ME FEELING DISAPPOINTED.
TSUKUMO, RIGHT NOW YOU'RE LIKE I WAS.
DON'T WORRY ABOUT OR CRY OVER SUCH THINGS AS...
...WHETHER TO TRANS-FORM OR WHETHER YOU'RE A PUP.

JOIN ME!
THERE ARE MANY HAPPY THINGS IN THE WORLD WE DON'T KNOW ABOUT!
LET'S GO SEE THEM TOGETHER!

...
Y...
SLASH
Y-YOU IDIOT! YOU ACT LIKE IT'S NOTHING...
...BUT HOW CAN I DECIDE?! IDIOT!
SEE THE WORLD, HUH?
PWAAH
W-WELL, ANYWAY... THINK ABOUT IT.
OKAY...
LOOK, UM... COULD YOU GET ME SOME WATER? I'M THIRSTY...
OH... ...SURE. OKAY.
...
TMP TMP TMP

KOFF
THANKS TO THE CARE YOU'VE GIVEN ME THESE LAST FEW MONTHS...
...I FEEL MUCH BETTER.

THANK YOU.
IT... IT'S OKAY...
...
WELL THEN...
...I THINK IT'S TIME TO CARRY OUT OUR PLAN.
!
LILLY...
...YOU WERE BORN WITH A VERY SPECIAL ABILITY.

AS A RESULT, THEY PERSECUTED YOU AND MADE YOU FEEL ALIENATED.
YOU NEVER FELT YOU BELONGED.
I WILL CHANGE THAT FOR YOU.
WITH YOUR ABILITY TO TRANSFORM...
...AND CONTROL OTHERS...
...WE CAN DO ANY-THING.
TRUST ME.
LEND ME YOUR STRENGTH.

SIGH...
A JOURNEY...
I'M LEAVING IN FOUR DAYS.
MEET ME AT THE SIGNPOST IF YOU'RE COMING.
TODAY IS THE FOURTH DAY...
I TOLD MOM AND DAD...
YOU IDIOT! I CAN'T LET A PUP GO OFF LIKE THAT!
WHAM
BUT...
...IF THAT'S YOUR CHOICE, NO ONE CAN STOP YOU.
WE'LL MISS YOU, BUT...
...THIS IS AN ADMIRABLE PATH TO

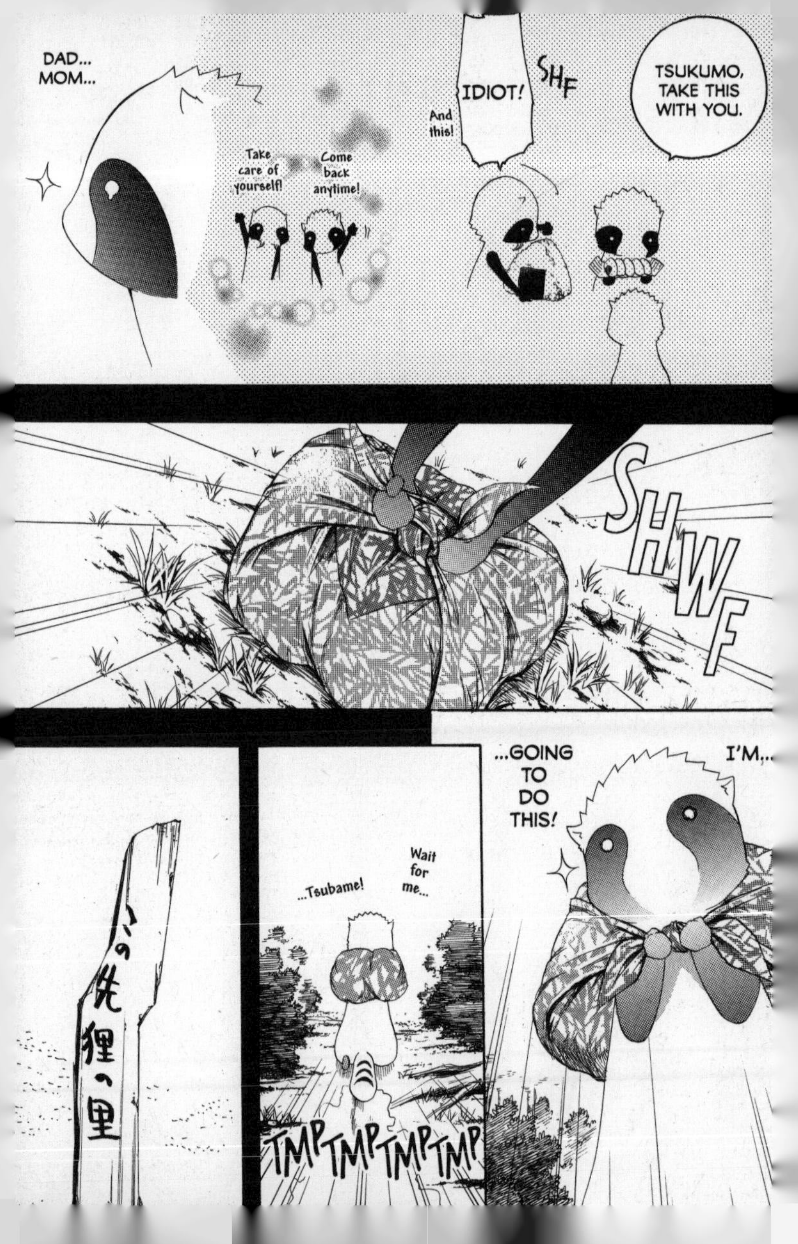
TSUKUMO, TAKE THIS WITH YOU.
SHF
IDIOT!
And this!
Come back anytime!
Take care of yourself!
DAD... MOM...
SHWF
I'M...
...GOING TO DO THIS!
Wait for me...
...Tsubame!
TMP TMP TMP TMP
この先狸の里

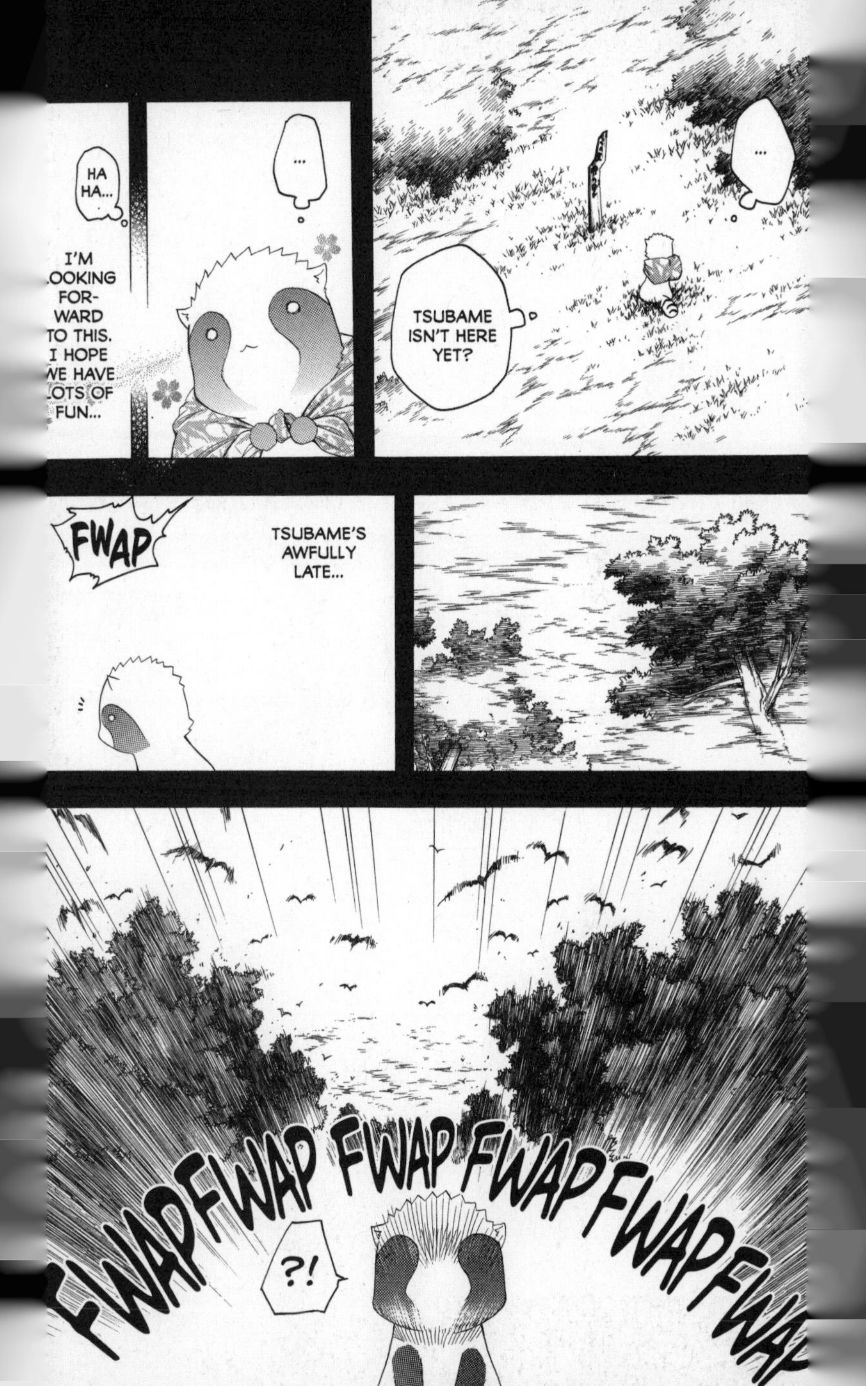

...
TSUBAME ISN'T HERE YET?
...
HA HA...
I'M LOOKING FOR-WARD TO THIS. I HOPE WE HAVE LOTS OF FUN...
TSUBAME'S AWFULLY LATE...
FWAP
FWAP FWAP FWAP FWAP FWAP FWAP FWAP
?!

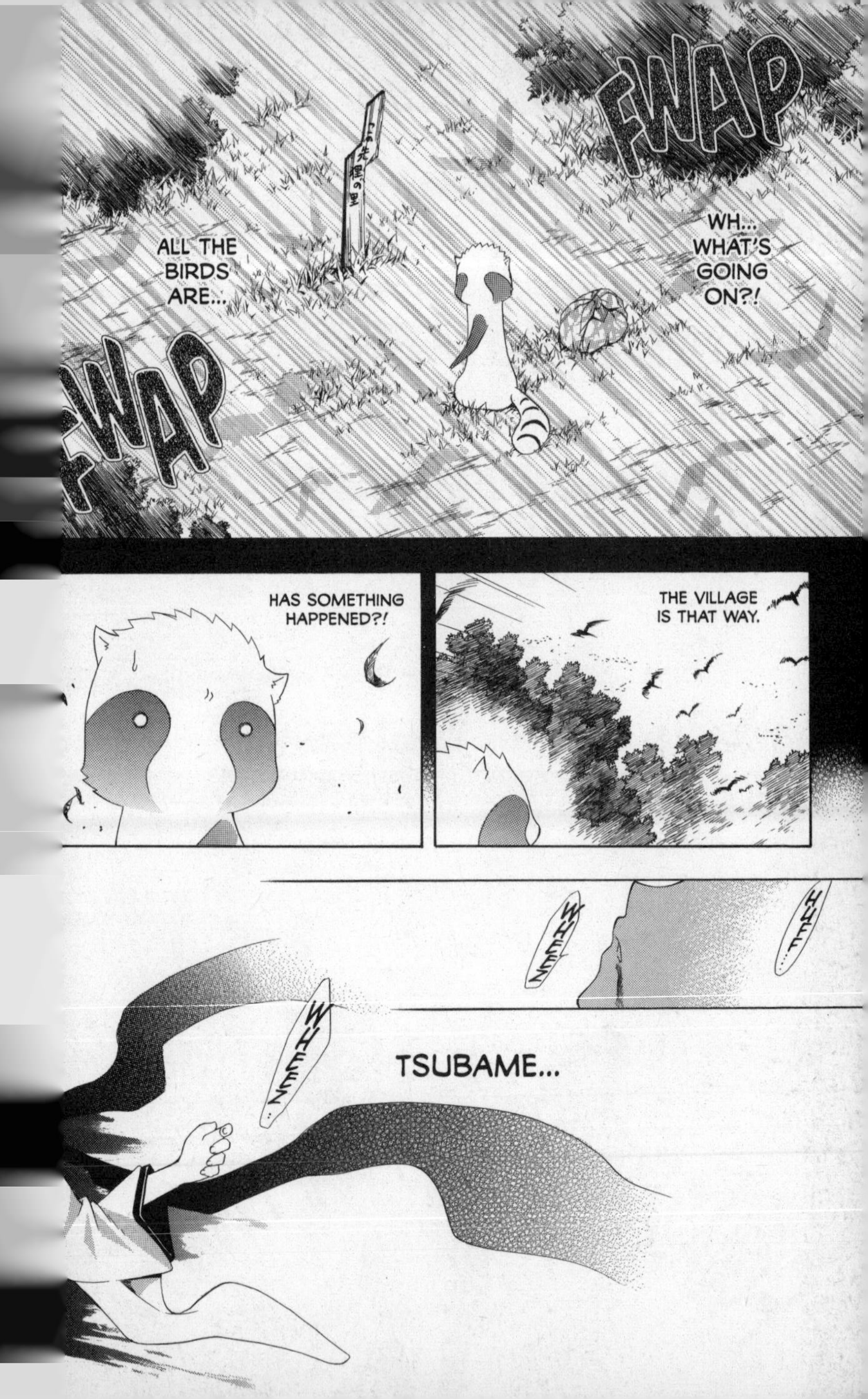
FWAP
WH... WHAT'S GOING ON?!
ALL THE BIRDS ARE...
FWAP
THE VILLAGE IS THAT WAY.
HAS SOMETHING HAPPENED?!
HUFF...
WHEEZ
WHEEZ..
TSUBAME...

HUFF
HUFF
DAD... MOM...
WHAT'S HAPPENED IN THE VILLAGE?
TSUBAME!
!
THE VILLAGE...
IT'S BEEN DE-STROYED!
A LAND-SLIDE? WAIT, WHAT...
HMM...
WHY DON'T YOU UNDER-STAND?

WITH YOUR POWER TO TRANSFORM...
...YOU DON'T NEED TO HIDE IN THE FOREST.
CASTLES, LANDS AND MONEY... YOU CAN HAVE IT ALL!
YOU JUST NEED TO COOPERATE WITH ME, THE WAY THESE TWO HAVE.
PSST
PSST
WHAT IS HE TALKING ABOUT?
WHO IS HE?
WHY ARE LILLY AND MAMI WITH HIM?
I SEE I'M NOT GETTING THROUGH TO YOU.
...
BUT IF I LET YOU GO, SOMEDAY YOU MAY RETURN TO THREATEN ME. I CAN'T AFFORD TO RUN THAT RISK.
THEREFORE, IN THE NAME OF TATSUHITO OGA...
...I WILL NOW EXTERMINATE YOU ALL!
?!

Chapter 123
Soul

GYAAAH!
FWUD
KYAAAAAAH
H-HE'S REALLY GONNA KILL US!
WAAAH
RUN!
HEY! WHAT'RE YOU DOING, TSUKUMO?! RUN!
THEY HAVE HUMAN WEAPONS!
...
THEY'RE GONNA KILL EVERYONE?
FOR NOT COOPERATING?
BUT... BUT...
HOW CAN THAT BE?!
HOW CAN YOU KILL OVER SOME-

SLASH

SKSSSSSH
PIPE DOWN, TSU-KUMO.
I'LL PUT YOU OUT OF YOUR MISERY SOON ENOUGH.
M... MAMI!

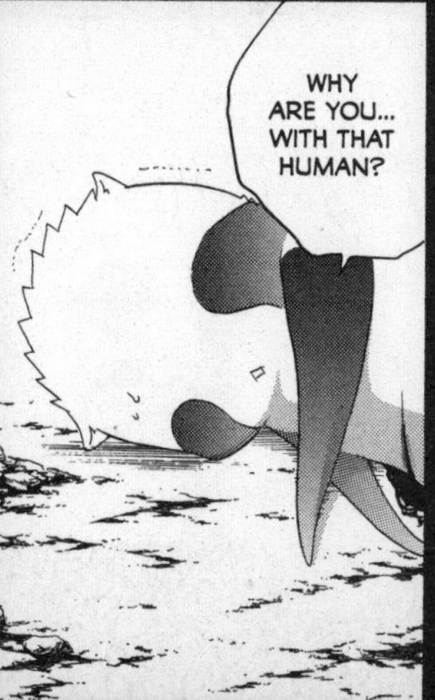
WHY ARE YOU... WITH THAT HUMAN?
......

...
I DO AS I PLEASE, TSUKUMO.
YOU DON'T NEED TO KNOW WHY.
AND NOW... GOODBYE.

GRB
!
!
GRRN
TANUKI ARE NO MATCH FOR HUMANS!
UNCLE...?
I TOLD YOU!
RUN!
BUT IF WE TRANSFORM, WE CAN SLOW THEM DOWN!
SHF
RUN! NOW!
HURRY!
C'MON! THIS WAY!
UNCLE!

I CAN'T BEAT THEM.

I CAN'T HELP ANYONE.

I CAN'T TRANSFORM.

I CAN'T DO...

...ANYTHING AT ALL!

HUH? UH... YEAH, I'M FINE.

I SHOULDN'T HAVE HAD TO USE THIS HUMAN WEAPON THOUGH.
I SHOULD'VE TRANSFORMED INTO SOMETHING BETTER.
LIKE A SWORD-MASTER OR A FELL BEAST! I CAN BECOME ANYTHING!
YES, THAT'S IMPRESSIVE, MAMI.
HEY! WANNA SEE ME TRANSFORM?
WHAT'S THE MATTER, MAMI?
WHUH?! NO, UH... IT'S NOTHING.
FOR NOW, I'D BETTER GO TO RYUBI.
HMM...
...
WHAT'S THE DEAL HERE? I CAN'T LEAVE THIS FORM...
IT STARTED WHEN I KILLED THAT TANUKI...
THE CURSE? BUT THAT WAS ONLY A RUMOR! THAT STORY ABOUT IT BEING FORBIDDEN CAN'T BE TRUE!

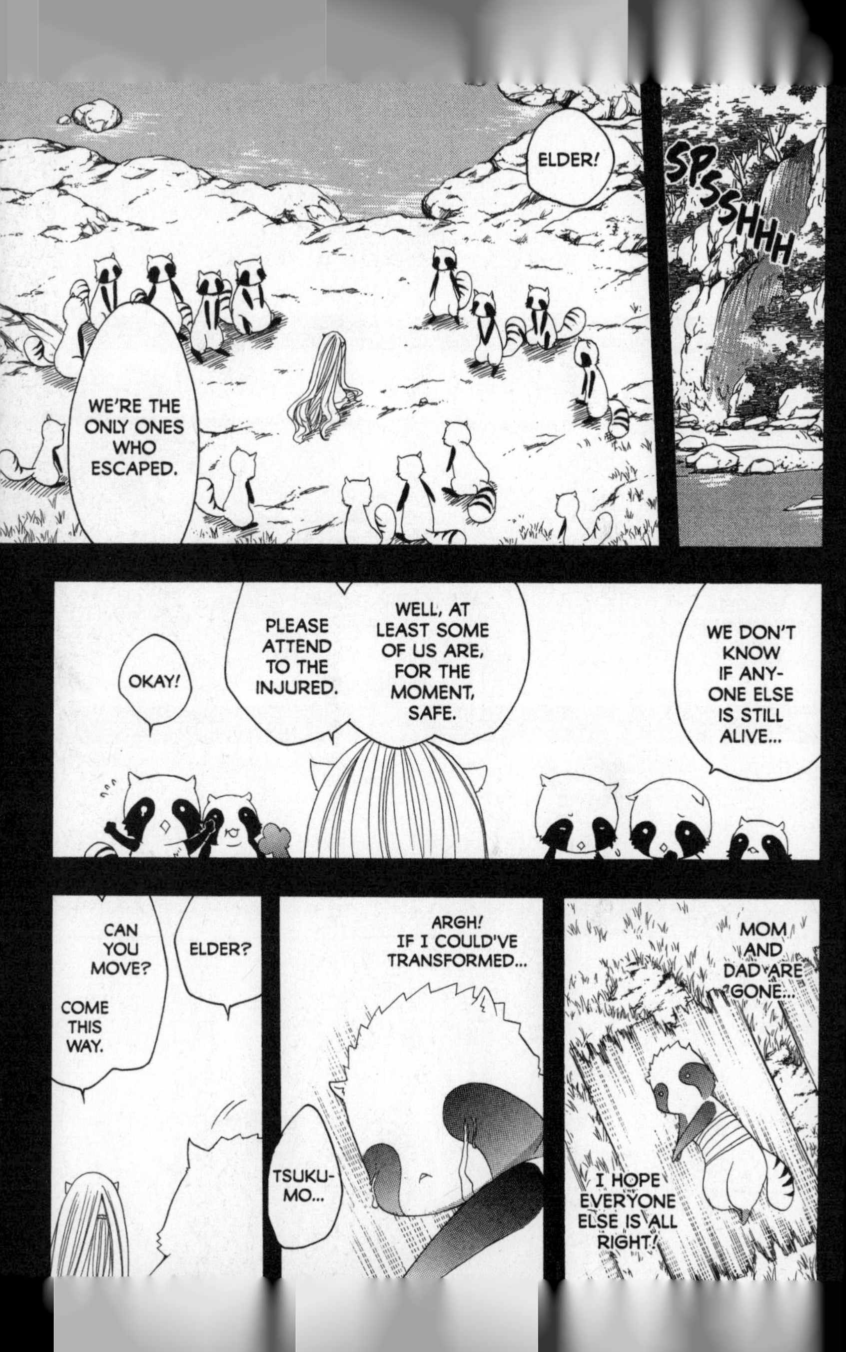
SPSSHHH
ELDER!
WE'RE THE ONLY ONES WHO ESCAPED.
WE DON'T KNOW IF ANY-ONE ELSE IS STILL ALIVE...
WELL, AT LEAST SOME OF US ARE, FOR THE MOMENT, SAFE.
PLEASE ATTEND TO THE INJURED.
OKAY!
MOM AND DAD ARE GONE...
I HOPE EVERYONE ELSE IS ALL RIGHT!
ARGH! IF I COULD'VE TRANSFORMED...
TSUKU-MO...
ELDER?
CAN YOU MOVE?
COME THIS WAY.

SOMEONE WANTS TO SEE YOU.
HE HELPED THE VILLAGERS ESCAPE FROM THE LANDSLIDE OUR ATTACKERS CAUSED.
THANKS TO HIM, THEY AVOIDED THE WORST OF IT.
HOW-EVER...
RUSTLE

TSUKUMO...
TSU...
TSU-BAME...
HELPED THE VILLAGERS ESCAPE FROM THE LANDSLIDE...
HE'S LOST...
...HIS FEET...
JOIN ME!
LET'S GO SEE THE WORLD TOGETHER!
BUT NOW...
...IT CAN'T BE.
GUESS OUR PLANS ARE OFF.

SORRY ABOUT THAT.
AND AFTER ALL THE THINGS I PROMISED...
BUT TSUBAME! IT'LL BE FINE! I MEAN...
NO, THAT'S ALL RIGHT.
TRUTH IS, I WASN'T GOING TO LIVE MUCH LONGER ANYWAY.
I'VE BEEN MEANING TO ASK YOU SOMETHING.
WHEN YOU CHANGE INTO SOMEONE...
...DO YOU ASSUME THEIR INJURIES OR SICKNESSES?
N... NO.
JUST THE ESSENTIAL FORM...
...AND ABILITIES...
AH...
GLAD TO HEAR THAT.
HEY, TSUKUMO?

HOW 'BOUT I GIVE YOU...
...MY SOUL.
!
IF IT'S YOU, I DON'T MIND.
BUT... THAT'S CRAZY!
YOU'RE NOT DYING YET!
YOU'RE GOING WITH ME!
TO FIND...
...HAP-PINESS AND... AND...
REMEMBER WHAT I TOLD YOU?
I'VE BEEN THROUGH SOME TOUGH TIMES.

I SPENT A LONG TIME ON BATTLE-FIELDS.
KILLING WAS COMMONPLACE... I WAS ALWAYS DRENCHED IN BLOOD.
I COULD HAVE LEFT, BUT I HAD SKILLS...
I FOUND WORK ALL OVER...
...AND DID A LOT OF KILLING.
BUT...
...MY EARS ARE SHARP, SO...
...IT GOT TO WHERE I COULDN'T STAND...
...HEARING THE GROANS AND CURSES AND HATE...
EVENTUALLY I COULDN'T EVEN STAND MYSELF.
IT WAS AWFUL...
NOTHING GOOD COMES FROM KILLING.
I JUST WANTED A LIFE THAT WOULD LET ME SMILE.

SO I STARTED COLLECTING THE KOKONOTSU...

...IN ORDER TO ATTAIN THE TREASURE OF GOD THAT GRANTS ANYTHING.

SINCE COMING HERE I'VE...

...SMILED ENOUGH FOR A LIFETIME!

KOFF
KOFF
TSUBAME!
!
TSUKUMO... I'M SORRY I CAN'T KEEP MY PROMISE.
HERE...
FWIK
I'D LIKE YOU TO HAVE THESE. KEEP THEM...
RE-MEM-BER ME...
...
TSU-BAME?

HEY...
TSU-
BAME?
TSU-
BAME!

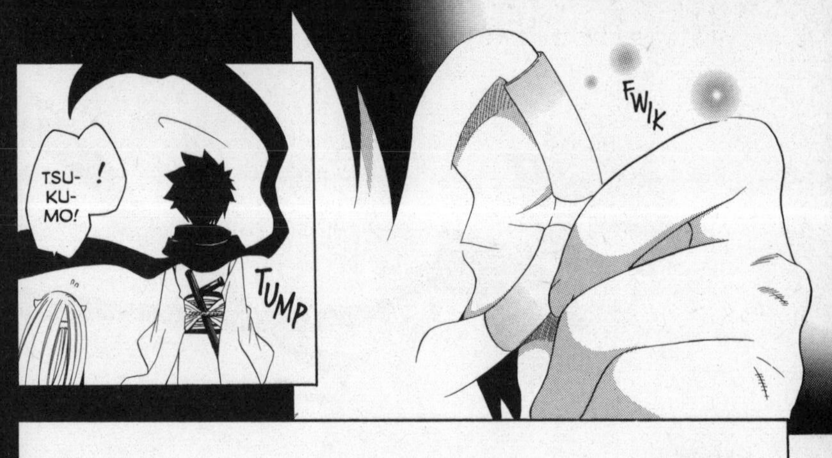

I PROMISE YOU THIS...

...TSUBAME.

THIS VILLAGE YOU LOVED SO MUCH...

...I WILL NOW PROTECT WITH MY LIFE!

TUMP
TUMP TUMP
WOW...
THIS BODY IS AMAZING!
IT'S A HUMAN BODY...
...BUT IT'S LIGHT AND FAST!
I'M OVERFLOWING WITH STRENGTH!
I HAD SKILLS...
THAT BARELY BEGINS TO DESCRIBE IT. THIS BODY IS INCREDIBLE, TSUBAME!
WITH THIS...

KRUMBL
...I SHOULD BE ABLE...
TMP TMP
TMP
TMP
IIID
SKIII
...TO FACE...
...TA-TSUHITO OGA...
...AND...
...KILL HIM!!
TUMP
!

Chapter 124
Forbidden

I CAN NEVER TURN INTO A TANUKI AGAIN.

WELL, SO WHAT?

IN EXCHANGE FOR THE POWER TO TRANSFORM, I GAINED *THIS* POWER.

AND THIS POWER WILL HELP HIM!

DON'T INTER-FERE...
...LILLY.
I CAN'T LET YOU GO TO HIM.
NO MATTER WHAT YOU DO...
...YOU CAN'T STOP ME.
FWIP
WHAM

...!
I DIDN'T SEE HIM...
SHWOOM
IF LILLY CHANGES INTO ME, SHE'LL CONTROL MY BODY.
BUT IT TAKES HER A LITTLE TIME TO TRANSFORM.
BEFORE SHE CAN DO THAT...
HWIP
CHOP
WHA WHAM
TOMP
THE ELDER WILL DECIDE YOUR PUNISHMENT LATER.
I DON'T KILL OTHER TANUKI.
I'LL ONLY KILL...

...HIM.
TATSUHITO OGA!
THE VILLAGE...
THE VILLAGERS...
TSUBAME...
IT'S ALL...
...HIS FAULT!
OGAAAAAA!!

IF IT WEREN'T FOR YOU...

WHOMP
KOFF
DIE, HUMAN!
KKK...
...OFFF
NO... YOU ARE...
...TSU-KUMO.
...?!
HOW DOES HE KNOW MY NAME?

!
POOOF
TSU... KU...
...MO...
HUH?
DAD...?

VWAH
WHAT...
...THE...?
GAAAAAH
MP
GW
...?!
IT'S GONE!
WHAT WAS THAT? NO...
WHAT ABOUT DAD?!
TSUKUMO MUJINA. GROVEL.

SLAM
?!!
TMP
AW...
POOR TSUKUMO. NOW YOU'RE LIKE ME.
YOU CAN'T RETURN TO BEING A TANUKI.
YOUR BODY IS CURSED.

YOU!
STILL, IF I HADN'T PREPARED A BODY DOUBLE, YOU'D HAVE KILLED ME.
BODY DOUBLE ?!
LUCKILY, I HAD YOUR FATHER ON HAND FOR THE PURPOSE.
I MET A COUPLE OF TANUKI EARLIER AND SAID I WOULD SPARE THE WIFE'S LIFE...
...IF HE WOULD CHANGE INTO MY FORM AND STAND THERE, AND HE MEEKLY OBEYED.
I KILLED THE FEMALE RIGHT AWAY...
...BUT HE DIDN'T KNOW THAT.
!!
TANUKI ARE FAR TOO TRUST- ING.
DIDN'T I TELL YOU?

I AM...

...AN ITSU-WARIBITO.

ITSU-WARI-BITO?!

I SURVIVE BY TELLING LIES.

NOT EVERYTHING HAS GONE QUITE ACCORDING TO PLAN, BUT SHALL WE CONTINUE? IT WON'T TAKE LONG TO KILL THE SURVIVORS.

SURE!

!

A CURSE FOR KILLING YOUR OWN KIND...
FORBIDDEN POWER...
THE SAME POWER...
I HAVE THE SAME POWER...
THEN WHAT I NEED IS...
"TSUKUMO MUJINA. GROVEL."
...A NAME?!
NO, MAYBE NOT...
BUT RIGHT NOW I HAVE TO RISK IT!

TATSUHITO... OGA!

!
UH-OH!
HE SAID TATSUHITO'S NAME!

?
MUJINA TSUKU-MO!
CLOSE YOUR MOU-

TURN TO STONE!
UNABLE TO MOVE, SPEND FOREVER REGRETTING!
TMP
MAMI...?
...
TA-TSUHI-TO?
TCH

!
HE'S FEELS HARD!
LIKE STONE...
IS HE BREATHING? IS THERE A PULSE?
IS HIS HEART BEATING?!
IS HE CONSCIOUS?
IS HE ALIVE? IS HE EVEN THERE?!
H-HOW DARE YOU!
UNDO THE CURSE!
ONLY YOU WHO CAST IT CAN UNDO IT!
WHY ON EARTH WOULD I DO THAT?
I WILL ***NEVER*** FORGIVE HIM FOR WHAT HE'S DONE!
...!
I CAN'T ORDER HIM TO UNDO IT.
BEFORE I COULD ORDER HIM, HE WOULD ORDER *ME*.
IF WE KILLED EACH OTHER...
...THEN NO ONE COULD EVER SAVE TATSUHITO.
TSU-KUMO, YOU-
WAIT, LILLY. IT'S ALL RIGHT.
MAMI?
WE SHOULD GO. WE DON'T KNOW ENOUGH ABOUT THE CURSED POWER.
WE'LL LOOK FOR A WAY TO SAVE TATSUHITO.
BUT REMEMBER, TSUKUMO...

SOMEDAY I WILL SAVE TATSUHITO...

...AND COME TO KILL YOU.

WHSH

WHETHER IT TAKES YEARS OR DECADES!

DAD... MOM... EVERYONE...

Chapter 125 Suggestion

I DON'T WANT SYM-PATHY.

WHAT'S IMPORTANT IS WHAT HAPPENS NEXT.

YES.
RYUBI LEFT AND YOU'RE RIGHT HERE. AT THE TIME...
...NEITHER OF YOU COULD MOVE BECAUSE OF THE CURSE, BUT NOW YOU CAN.

AND THEREIN LIES THE ANSWER...

THERE MUST BE A WAY TO BREAK THE SPELL.
AND FOR ME TO DIE...

Chapter 125
Suggestion

...
I THINK YOU ALREADY HAVE AN IDEA.
AND WHEN IT COMES TO LILLY'S ABILITY...
...MUCH IS UNCLEAR...
...BUT...
...SHE BASICALLY COMMANDS ALL OUR SENSES, IDEAS AND INTENTIONS.
LIKE A STRONG *SUGGESTION*.
!
SUGGES-TION?!

LIKE TANUKI POWERS, SOME THINGS ARE UNEXPLAINABLE.
Such as how reliable it is...
I THINK THE ROOT OF IT IS CONVINCING YOUR OPPONENT OF SOMETHING.
SAYING THE OPPONENT'S NAME GETS THEIR ATTENTION.
YOU'RE RIGHT.
AND COMMANDING SOMETHING PHYSICALLY IMPOSSIBLE DOESN'T ENABLE THE SUBJECT TO ACTUALLY DO IT.
X CAN'T FLY.
Fly!!
O JUST TRIES TO FLY.
A FEW DECADES AGO, MAMI TOLD ME NOT TO MOVE.
IT TOOK QUITE SOME TIME, BUT I EVENTUALLY BROKE FREE OF THE SUGGESTION.
I STARTED BY USING MY OWN WORD ABILITY TO MOVE ONE FINGER.
Move! Move! Move!
You can do it!
Took care of him for a long time.
THIS POWER IS NOT ABSOLUTE. IT IS POSSIBLE TO BREAK.
IT'S PARTIALLY A MENTAL CHALLENGE, SO IT TAKES TIME...
...AND SOMETIMES IT MAY LAST FOR LIFE.
...
UM...
Just guess-ing...
DOES THAT MEAN...

LILLY CAN TAKE HER OPPONENT'S FORM AND CONTROL IT BY ISSUING A VISUAL SUGGESTION.

POINTING WITH A FINGER OR SHOWING WORDS IS ENOUGH.

Uzume, say "Ooh!"

OOH!

BESIDES, CAN YOU FIGHT WITH YOUR EYES CLOSED OR YOUR EARS PLUGGED?

OOOH ...

THERE IS ONLY ONE WAY TO ESCAPE.

AND THAT IS TO BE UNAWARE THAT THE SUGGES-TION IS FOR ***YOU***.

HOW... WOULD THAT WORK?

LET'S SAY YOU CHANGED YOUR NAME. A COMMAND UNDER YOUR OLD NAME WOULDN'T REGISTER.
NOW THAT I THINK ABOUT IT, WHEN MAMI FACED ME EARLIER AND I CALLED HER NAME, SHE DIDN'T REACT.
MAMI!
MAKES ME THINK SHE CHANGED HER NAME AND MADE IT HER OWN.

BUT YOU CAN'T INTERNALIZE A NEW NAME OVERNIGHT.
WE JUST DON'T HAVE TIME FOR THAT.

NO, WE DON'T.
BUT THERE IS SOME-THING WE CAN DO.

THE KEY IS UZUME.

AND CHIT-CHORIINA.
YOU TWO.

EH? WHADDA YA MEAN?
WHAT'RE WE GONNA DO?
Hmm...
It won't hurt them, will it?
CHITCHO-RIINA, I'D RATHER NOT INVOLVE YOU...

...BUT YOUR NAME AS RECORDED IN THE REGISTRY...
...WAS YOUR NICKNAME OF POCHI.

Oh...
I see...

THE CURSE DOESN'T WORK ON NICKNAMES.
THAT MEANS YOU'RE IMMUNE, THEY CAN'T COMMAND YOU.
BUT POCHI MIGHT OBEY ANYWAY...
FREEZE

AND UZUME...
YOU ONLY HAVE A FIRST NAME, RIGHT?

SO THINK OF A LAST NAME!
!
IT'S EASIER TO ADD A NAME THAN CHANGE ONE!

THAT WILL WEAKEN, AND PERHAPS NEGATE, THE CURSE'S EFFECT.
EITHER WAY, YOU CAN PUT UP A FIGHT!

MAKE UP A LAST NAME? JUST LIKE THAT?
INSTEAD OF MAKING IT UP, WHY NOT USE ONE YOU KNOW?
ONE YOU MIGHT EVEN LIKE TO HAVE.
THAT I'D LIKE...

HOW ABOUT *AZAKO*?
UZUME AZAKO!
How do you write Azako?
TAKE KAWAZU!
OR MUITO!
OR YAKUMA!

ACTUALLY, CHOZA, THE MOST REASON-ABLE ONE WOULD BE YOUR LAST NAME.
MINE? THAT WOULD BE STUPID!

THEN AGAIN, I GUESS IT WOULD BE OKAY...
HOW ABOUT YASHIMA?
Nibyo!

SO MANY
NAMES
Muito
Yakuma
Kawazu
Azako
Yashima
Habaki

BUT...
Hee hee! Which should I choose? Which is best?
KAWA-ZU.

...WE ALSO HAVE TO DEAL WITH LILLY'S VISUAL SUG-GESTIONS.
FOR THOSE, I MIGHT...

...JUST HAVE...
...AN IDEA THAT COULD WORK.

CARE TO ENLIGHTEN US?
NOT YET. IT'S AN IDEA, NOT A PLAN.

OH BOY...

...?

BY THE WAY, UTSUHO...

WHAT DID YOU MEAN SHE COULD KILL ME?
SHE COULD ?!
IF SHE MADE ME STAB OR STRANGLE MYSELF...
...I STILL WOULDN'T DIE.
...
HAVE YOU HEARD OF...
...HYPNOSIS?
HYPNOSIS?
WELL... I GUESS IT DEPENDS ON HOW YOU DEFINE DEATH, BUT...
...IN A CERTAIN COUNTRY, THEY USE A STRONG SUGGESTION...
...ON PRISONERS ON DEATH ROW TO CAUSE THEM TO DIE. SELF-EXECUTION, YOU MIGHT SAY.

A SUG-GESTION TO ***DIE***?

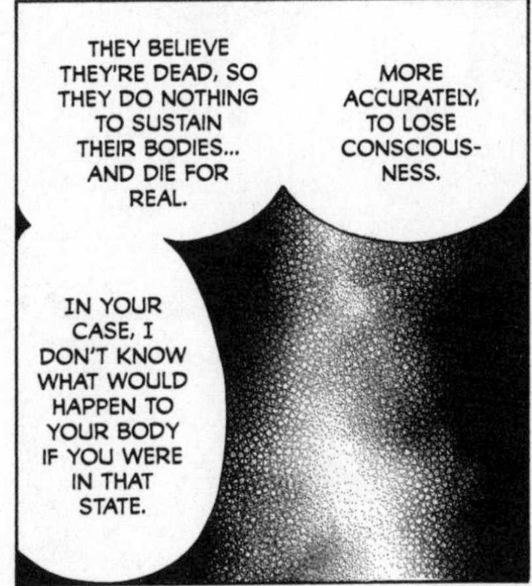
MORE ACCURATELY, TO LOSE CONSCIOUS-NESS.
THEY BELIEVE THEY'RE DEAD, SO THEY DO NOTHING TO SUSTAIN THEIR BODIES... AND DIE FOR REAL.
IN YOUR CASE, I DON'T KNOW WHAT WOULD HAPPEN TO YOUR BODY IF YOU WERE IN THAT STATE.

IF YOU THOUGHT YOU WERE DEAD AND WENT ON THINKING SO...
...WOULDN'T THAT BE THE SAME AS DYING?
...

HMM...
MUMBLE MUMBLE
IF I STOPPED THINKING OR PERCEIVING OR DREAMING AND THAT CONTINUED FOREVER...
...THAT WOULD BE LIKE DEATH.
...
...

WELL, WE EACH HAVE OUR IDEAS...
...BUT OUR OPTIONS ARE STILL LIMITED.

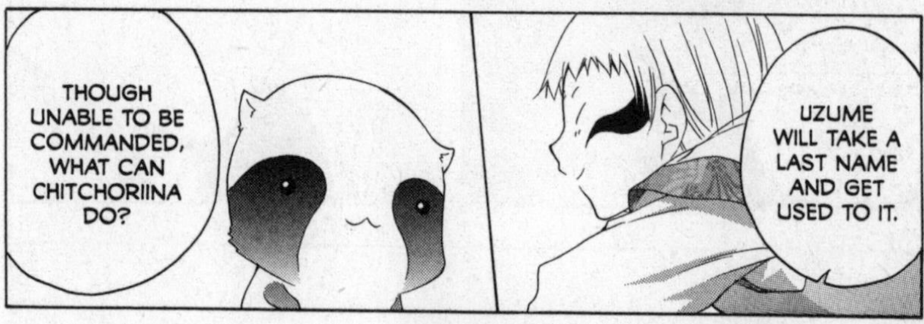
UZUME WILL TAKE A LAST NAME AND GET USED TO IT.
THOUGH UNABLE TO BE COMMANDED, WHAT CAN CHITCHORIINA DO?

RYUBI HAS THAT REGIS-TRY.
HE'S NO FOOL. HE'LL SOON HAVE THOSE NAMES SORTED OUT.
GIVEN THAT, HOW CAN WE FIGHT BACK?

YET WE MUST. WE CANNOT LET THEM GO.

THIS TIME, WE'VE GOT TO ***WIN***.

OKAY, SO MOST OF US ARE HAMSTRUNG BECAUSE OF THIS NAME THING.

DON'T FORGET THAT OTHER THING, CHOZA.
Umph!
WHAT OTHER THING?
YOUR TATTOO.
HUNH?
ONE OF THE ENEMY GOT AWAY BECAUSE OF IT.
SHE COULD HAVE KILLED YOU.
SO I THINK...

...YOU NEED TO GET OVER HOW YOU FEEL LETTING PEOPLE SEE IT.
I'LL HELP YOU.
NO.
QUICK AN-SWER!
WHY NOT? IT'S TIME, DON'TCHA THINK?
BUT IF I DON'T WANNA, I DON'T WANNA! I WON'T, WON'T, WON'T!
ABSO-LUTELY NOT!
IT'S... IT'S *IMPOS-SIBLE!*
WHY? YOU'RE FINE WHEN I SEE IT!
YEAH! BUT JUST YOU!
C'MON, TRY!
NUH-UH!
SPSSHHH

ARE YOU...
...MAKING PROGRESS?

Hikae Nibyo
YES, I THINK SO.
BUT THEY OUT-NUMBER US.
SO I HAVE A FAVOR TO ASK YOU TWO.
GO TO THEM WITH AN INVITATION.
FROM WHAT I'VE SEEN...
...SOME OF THEM MIGHT WANT TO JOIN US.

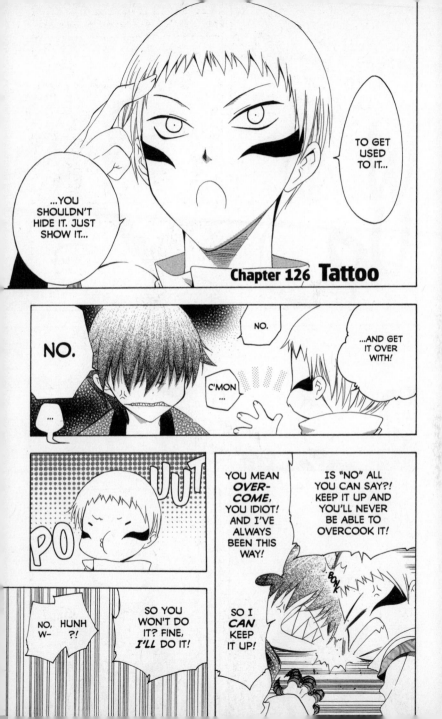

TO GET USED TO IT...

...YOU SHOULDN'T HIDE IT. JUST SHOW IT...

Chapter 126 Tattoo

...AND GET IT OVER WITH!
C'MON ...
NO.
NO.
...

IS "NO" ALL YOU CAN SAY?! KEEP IT UP AND YOU'LL NEVER BE ABLE TO OVERCOOK IT!

YOU MEAN *OVERCOME*, YOU IDIOT! AND I'VE ALWAYS BEEN THIS WAY!

BONK

SO I *CAN* KEEP IT UP!

POUT

SO YOU WON'T DO IT? FINE, *I'LL* DO IT!

HUNH ?!

NO, W-

WUP

CHATTER
CHATTER
He isn't moving...
I could doodle on him!
No!
HEY, DON'T DO THAT! YOU'RE INTRUDING ON HIM AND...
...AND...

STOP ...
...THAT...

STOP...
...THAT...
STOP ...
... THAT ...
STOP THAT, STOP THAT, STOP THAT...
...STOP THAT!
PLIP
PLIP
PLIP

GET YOUR...
GRB

...HANDS OFF ME!
SLAM

GRB

CUT THE NON-SENSE!
I SAID I'M NOT DOING IT!
TRY THAT AGAIN...

...AND I'LL **KILL** YOU!

YOU GET ME?
NO... WAIT... YOU... DON'T ACT SO SURPRISED!
DON'T MAKE THAT FACE! DON'T ACT SO SCARED!
NOW I FEEL LIKE *I* WAS WRONG! BUT WHO'S THE VICTIM HERE? YOU?!

UZUME IS WORRIED ABOUT YOU.
BUT HIS WAY OF SHOWING IT SUCKS.
WELL, THAT'S IMPOR-TANT!
Don't be so soft on Uzume!
I hope he's okay...
GRAH GRAH

Chapter 126
Tattoo

HOO
CHATTER
CHATTER
TUMP
UTSU-HO...
SPSSHHHH
YOU'RE ALONE? THAT'S UNUSUAL.
WHERE'S POCHI?
AT GRAND-FATHER'S.
POCHI SAYS IT'S FUN TALKING ABOUT HIS MOM.
YAKU-MA?
DOES POCHI'S GRANDFATHER STILL INSIST POCHI STAY HERE?
YEAH...

OH WELL...
IT'S GOOD TO HAVE A REAL FAMILY.
OH?
I MEAN, POCHI AND I ARE FAMILY...
...BUT REAL FAMILY... YOUR OWN BLOOD... THAT'S DIFFERENT.
I WAS SO HAPPY WHEN I HAD A MOTHER AND FATHER.
WHEN I LOST THEM, SO MUCH CHANGED. I STILL HAVEN'T GOTTEN OVER IT, NOT COMPLETELY.
UTSUHO...
IS HE PONDERING THE POSSIBILITY OF LEAVING POCHI HERE?
YES...

THAT WILL BE...
...THE KEY TO DEFEATING THEM THIS TIME.
GRIN
?!
UH...
UT-SUHO... YOU'RE NOT...
EH? WHAT?
YOU'RE NOT FEELING SAD?
SAD?
WHY *WOULD* I BE?
YOU KNOW, ABOUT RETURNING POCHI TO...
RETURN POCHI?!

"RETURN" POCHI?! I'M NOT JUST WATCHING HIM!
I'M NOT A DAY-CARE!
AM I A DAYCARE ?!
OKAY, BUT MINAMO PREDICTED IT, AND AFTER...
YOU AND THAT CHILD... ...WILL SEPARATE.
...WE HEARD ABOUT TSUKUMO'S FAMILY...
...I JUST THOUGHT MAYBE YOU-
JAB
JAB
I WAS THINKING ABOUT BEATING THE ENEMY AND HAVING GRANDFATHER RECOGNIZE ME AND POCHI!
OH.
And the treasure?
POCHI AND ME AREN'T TANUKI FAMILY, WE'RE TANUKI-HUMAN FAMILY... A NEW FAMILY!
And I'll get the treasure!
UH... NEW FAMILY?
YOU KNOW, A MAN TAKES A BRIDE...
A BRIDE ?!
...OR A WOMAN TAKES A GROOM...
GROOM ?!
...AND THEY SETTLE DOWN TO-GETHER.
OY!
POCHI AND ME ARE LIKE THAT.
GOT IT?
UH...
NO!

BUT I GUESS IT DEPENDS ON WHAT POCHI WANTS.
WELL, SHALL WE GO BACK?
HEY... UTSUHO?
I FORGOT TO ASK ABOUT LILLY. HOW DOES HE PLAN TO BEAT HER POWER?
AND LOSING FAMILY AND THINGS CHANGING... HOW ARE THEY KEY?
KOSHIRO.
TSU-KUMO?
EVERY-ONE'S RESTING.
YOU MUST BE TIRED TOO.
IS YOUR HAND ALL RIGHT?
YEAH, IT'S FULLY HEALED. NO PROBLEM. THANKS FOR ASKING.
HOW'S YOURS?

A SUG-GESTION...

...THAT COULD KILL ME...

IF WHAT UTSUHO SAYS IS TRUE, I WOULD DIE.

BUT IF THAT'S THE CASE...

KITTY-BOY!

NIBYO-SAN!

HIME! AND POCHI?
I HEARD YOU WERE ON GUARD, SO I BROUGHT A LATE-NIGHT SNACK!
Woohoo!
REALLY? GREAT! THANKS!
YOU MUST BE PRETTY LONELY OUT HERE.
NO, NOT REALLY.
I DON'T SLEEP ANYWAY.
MM-MM!
I'D BE BORED IF IT WEREN'T FOR GUARD DUTY.
YOU DON'T SLEEP?
YEAH. IT'S A SIDE EFFECT OF THIS IMMORTAL BODY.
I DON'T SLEEP, OR CAN'T. SAME THING, I GUESS.
OH DEAR...
HA HA! QUITE A PROBLEM, RIGHT?
I'M ALMOST A MONSTER!
FM

HMM... UM...
NOT HAVING TO SLEEP MUST BE NICE.
I GET SLEEPY AT NINE O'CLOCK...
YAWN
YOU GONNA SLEEP HERE?
GUARDING DOESN'T SEEM HARD...
...BUT STILL KIND OF LONELY...
ZZZ
She fell asleep?
POCHI HELP GUARD TOO...
ZZZZ
Pochi too!
...

GOD...
...WHAT SHOULD I DO?
I THINK...
...I'M REALLY HAPPY RIGHT NOW.
THAT'S A PROBLEM...
A PROBLEM INDEED...
HEY, GOD?
I...
...
COME OUT ALREADY.
GASP
CHOZA...
...ARE YOU STILL MAD?
Unh...
HUH? NO, OF COURSE NOT. WHY WOULD I BE?
Your stupidity always annoys me, but...

IT'S NOT LIKE I DON'T WANT TO FIX THIS.
IF POSSIBLE, I DO WANT TO GET OVER IT.
EVEN IF YOU CAN'T RIGHT NOW...
...I HOPE YOU CAN SOMEDAY.
I JUST...
...DON'T WANT YOU TO DIE.
...
I KNOW.
BUT IT'S AN EMO-TIONAL PROBLEM.
THINGS LIKE THAT AREN'T EASY TO SOLVE.
YEAH...
I UNDER-STOOD THAT...
...WHEN I HEARD ABOUT TSUKUMO.

HIS FAMILY...
...WAS KILLED...
...DECADES AGO, AND IN ALL THAT TIME...
...THE HATE HE FEELS BECAUSE OF THAT HASN'T GONE AWAY. IT STILL MARKS HIM.
I ALSO THINK...
...I'M THE SORT OF PERSON HE HAS A RIGHT TO HATE.
...
THAT MAY BE TRUE, I DON'T KNOW.
FOR-GIVE-NESS ISN'T EASY.
YOU SUFFERED FOR SO LONG...
...AND SAW YOUR COMRADES KILLED.
YEAH, BUT I...
...AVENGED THEM, INCLUDING KUROHA...
...SO FORGIVING THEIR KILLERS ISN'T A QUESTION.

I DON'T MEAN THEM.
I MEAN BANDA.
BANDA?
WHEN HE WAS KILLED, YOU WERE FAIRLY READY FOR IT...
...AND ACCEPTED IT CALMLY.

HE WAS YOUR DEAR COMRADE TOO.

MAYBE YOU ACCEPTED IT...
...BUT WHAT IF THE KILLER APPEARED BEFORE YOU?
GASP
BANDA'S ...
UH-OH! UZUME DIDN'T KNOW!
...KILL-ER?
THAT'S RIGHT...
WHEN BANDA DIED...

HUH?
THERE'S THIS OTHER WEIRD GUY...
...AND HE KILLED HIM.
...THAT'S WHAT CHOZA SAID.
UZUME DIDN'T KNOW EXACTLY WHO KILLED HIM!
WHO WAS IT?
WHO KILLED BANDA?
UZUME...
IF YOU DON'T TELL ME, I'LL ASK SOMEONE ELSE.
...
CAT-EYES...
...DID IT.
CAT-EYES...
HE KILLED BANDA!

YOU NEED TO TALK?

Chapter 127 Sweet Invitation

...

IT'S ABOUT LILLY'S POWER.

WHEN SHE TRANSFORMS...

PAWOOF

...WHAT HAPPENS TO HER ALSO HAPPENS TO THE PERSON SHE'S COPYING.

PINCH

BUT THE REVERSE IS ALSO TRUE.

WHEN LILLY CHANGES INTO SOMEONE...

...AND SOMETHING HAPPENS TO THE OTHER PERSON...

...IT HAPPENS TO LILLY AS WELL.

!

YOU MEAN TO SAY-
YES.
I'LL SERVE AS DECOY...
...AND MAKE HER COPY ME.
THEN WHEN LILLY LOOKS LIKE ME...
...SOME-ONE CAN STAB AND KILL ME.
IF WE DO THAT, LILLY WILL SUFFER THE SAME WOUND.
BUT IF WE DO THAT, YOU'LL-
DON'T WORRY. I DON'T INTEND TO DIE.
I WANT TO TALK ABOUT WHAT COMES NEXT.

WHEN I'M DYING, I WANT YOU TO HEAL ME.

!

I KNOW IT'S A RISK, BUT IT'S A CHANCE TO MINIMIZE OUR CASUALTIES.

I CAN'T DO IT ALONE.

I CAN'T EVEN TAKE MAMI ON BY MYSELF.

BUT I MUST REFUSE.
I'M A DOCTOR, AND AS SUCH I SIMPLY CAN'T DO ANYTHING THAT RISKS LIFE.
...!
YOU HONOR ME BY THE TRUST YOU HAVE IN ME...
...BUT I WOULD ASK YOU TO TRUST MY COMPANIONS EQUALLY.
UTSU-HO...
...SAID HE MAY BE ABLE TO DO SOMETHING.
AND I BELIEVE HE *CAN*.
TRUST IN *THAT*.
...

BUT HE'S AN ITSUWARI-BITO...
A LYING HUMAN...
CLENCH

THAT'S TRUE, BUT NOT THE WHOLE STORY.
HE TELLS GOOD LIES.

FINE. SORRY I BOTHERED YOU, KOSHIRO.
TUMP
TSU-KU-MO...

I SHOULD HAVE CHANGED MY NAME TOO.
JUST LIKE THEY DID.
I HAD PLENTY OF TIME.

BUT I SUPPOSE YOU COULDN'T.
NAMES ARE GIVEN BY OUR PARENTS. THEY'RE IMPOR-TANT.
THEY'RE NOT EASY TO THROW AWAY. AND IN YOUR CASE...

...YOU RISK YOUR LIFE TO KEEP YOURS.
I THINK THAT'S ADMIRA-BLE.
TUMP TUMP
YAKU-MA!
...

NEYA? WHAT'S WRONG ?!
WELL...
...UZUME AND HIKAE ARE FIGHTING!
?!
Chapter 127
Sweet Invitation

WHAT'S UP? YOU LOOK SERIOUS.
I JUST HEARD...
...YOU KILLED BANDA. IS THAT TRUE?
BANDA?
OH!
I RE-MEMBER THAT GUY!
YEAH, I KILLED HIM. WHAT OF IT?
YOU WANT REVENGE?

...
HEY!
WHAT'S GOING ON?
TUMP

UM... NOTHING. NOT A THING.
IT'S JUST SOME... OLD BUSINESS.
OH...
UZUME ISN'T THAT DUMB. HE WOULDN'T SEEK REVENGE OUT OF LINGERING RESENTMENT.
HE COULDN'T STOP HIMSELF FROM CONFRONTING CAT-EYES...
...BUT NOW HE'S WONDERING IF HE CAN FORGIVE HIM...
...AND IS CONSIDERING HIS OWN PAST ACTIONS.

I NEEDED TO TELL HIM...
...BUT MY TIMING COULD'VE BEEN BETTER.
SEEMS I'M THE IDIOT THIS TIME.
CR
AK
...
WE NEED TO COOPERATE RIGHT NOW, BUT...

NIBYO, ARE YOU ALL RIGHT?
NEVER BETTER.
IN FACT, THIS IS RATHER OPPOR-TUNE.
Hmph!
HEY... WHERE'S UTSU-HO?
I'M HERE. YOU WANTED TO TALK?
YEAH... A LITTLE BIT.
I KNOW IT'S IMPORTANT TO YOU, BUT WOULD YOU CONSIDER...
...GIVING UP FINDING...
...THE KOKO-NOTSU?
...
HUH?

ARE YOU SERIOUS?
UTSUHO, I'M SURE YOU'RE SUSPICIOUS ABOUT THE TREASURE.
BUT YOU DON'T KNOW EXACTLY WHY...
...SO I'LL GIVE YOU A HINT.
IT'S A COMPLEX STORY...
AS I SAID, IT'S AN OLD, OLD STORY...
ONCE UPON A TIME, THERE WAS AN INCREDIBLY HONEST YOUTH.
THE HONEST PERSON IS A WOMAN.
BUT THEN...
...A LIAR SHOWED UP.
"YOUTH..."
"...WE PRAISE YOUR HEART, WHICH DOES NOT HATE THOUGH YOU'VE LOST EVERYTHING..."
THE LIAR SKILLFULLY CAJOLED THE YOUTH...
THE LIAR IS GOD.
...WITH MANY TWISTS AND TURNS, AS OUTSIDERS TELL IT.
WHAT IF NONE OF IT WERE TRUE?
NOT TRUE?
WHAT IF IT WAS A STORY SPREAD BY *LIARS*?
SEE WHAT I'M GETTING AT?
...AND THIS TREAS-URE OF GOD, REALLY?
WHAT IS GOD...

WHY SEARCH FOR SOME-THING SO VAGUE?
...
I SEE YOUR POINT.
EVERYTHING I KNOW ABOUT THE TREASURE IS BASED ON SPECULA-TION.
BUT ONE THING SEEMS CERTAIN...
THE TREASURE OF GOD EXISTS.
AND IT'S SOME-THING WITH INCREDIBLE POWER.
YOU AFFIRMED THAT YOURSELF.
AND WE HAVE REASONS FOR OBTAINING THE TREASURE.
SO I'LL KEEP GOING...
...NO MATTER WHAT IT LEADS TO.
...
OH...

ARE WE CLEAR?
HI-KAE?
YES. CLEAR AS A BELL. LATER.
...
OF COURSE.
HE WON'T STOP JUST BECAUSE I SUGGEST IT.
IT'S ALWAYS BEEN THAT WAY WITH HIM.
THE PROBLEM IS ME.
SHOULD I ROOT FOR HIM?
OR NOT?
OR...
RUSTLE
EH? AH...
IT'S YOU.
WHAT DO YOU WANT?

I WANT TO...
...TALK TO YOU.
YEAH? WHAT ABOUT?
CHOZA...
SORRY I WORRIED YOU.
YOU HAVE ENOUGH STUFF TO DEAL WITH.
I'M FINE, REALLY.
JUST DO WHAT YOU CAN ABOUT THAT STUFF WHEN YOU CAN, OKAY?
...
HE'S NOT SURE WHAT TO DO...

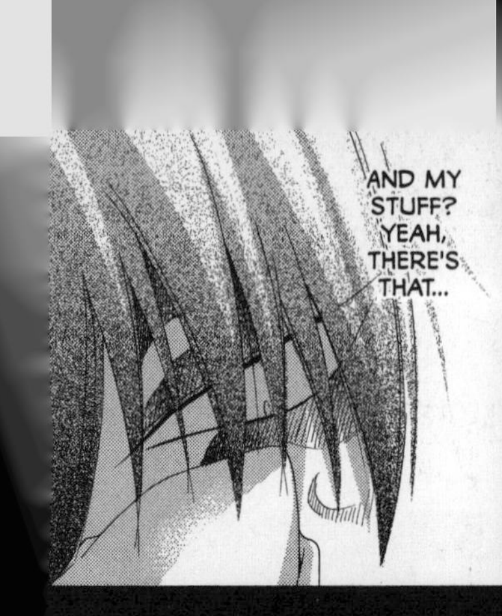

SHE COULD HAVE KILLED YOU.

I KNOW THAT.

THIS SITUATION ASIDE, I NEED TO DO SOMETHING ABOUT MY TATTOO.

ARGH! THE WHOLE THING'S SUCH A PAIN!

I MEAN, I ONCE TRIED BURNING MY WHOLE FACE!

I EVEN THOUGHT ABOUT PEELING ALL THE SKIN OFF!

BUT THEN I ALWAYS THINK...

WHY SHOULD I HAVE TO DO THAT?!

I WASN'T GIVEN THIS TATTOO BECAUSE OF A CRIME I COMMITTED.

DO I REALLY NEED TO WORRY SO MUCH ABOUT WHAT OTHERS THINK?!

IF THEY IRRITATE ME, I SHOULD JUST BEAT 'EM UP.

YOU!
WHSH
WAIT! STOP!
DON'T MAKE ME FLIP YOUR HAIR!
...
CALM DOWN. I DIDN'T COME TO FIGHT. I CAME TO TALK.
TALK?
YES.
YOU SEEM...
...QUITE WORRIED ABOUT THAT TATTOO.

WHAT WOULD YOU SAY...

!

INVITE ME?
YES.
YOU'RE WORRIED ABOUT SOME-THING.
I'LL GET RID OF IT FOR YOU.
IN RETURN ...
...I JUST WANT YOU...
...TO JOIN US.

◆ Bonus Manga ◆

GRANDFATHER, WOULD YOU TELL US WHAT POCHI'S PARENTS WERE LIKE?

HMM... WELL...
...THEY WERE BOTH SPLENDID TANUKI WITH PURE HEARTS.
THE WHOLE WORLD LOVED THEM.

THE MO- MENT...

...THE TWO MET...

...FLOWERS BLOOMED ...

...BIRDS SANG...

...THE WIND DANCED ...
..LIGHT FILLED THE AIR...

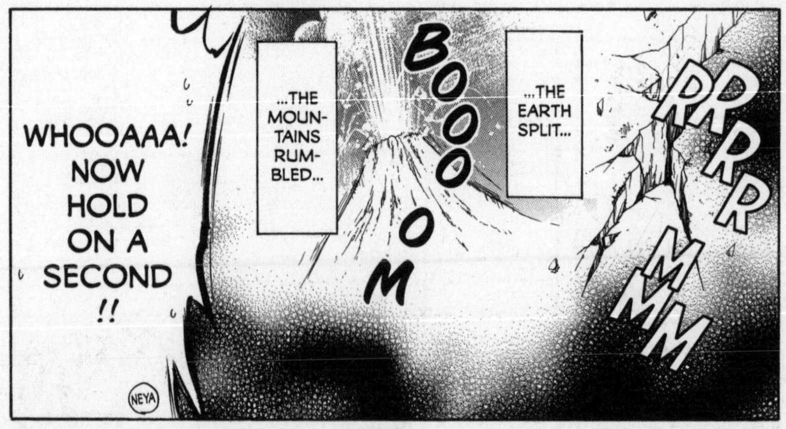
RRRRMMMM
...THE EARTH SPLIT...
BOOOOOM
...THE MOUNTAINS RUMBLED...
WHOOAAA! NOW HOLD ON A SECOND !!
NEYA

IN THE TANUKI VILLAGE...

THAT'S ONE OF THE HUMANS.
I'LL PLAY A LITTLE TRICK ON HIM...

POOF

CHOZA! DON'T SIT THERE!

THOSE FLOWERS ARE TOXIC!
WHAT?!
THEY'LL MAKE YOU GO BALD!
HUNH?! REALLY?!
MOVE ABOUT TO REMOVE THE POISON!
Dance!

I DON'T WANNA BE BALD!
GYAAAAH!
FLAP FLAP
...
BWA HA!

WA HA HA HA!
POOF
OH, FOR...
IT WAS A TRICK!

WAAAH! YOU TRICKED ME!
POOF

Oh, it was you?
You tricked me...
We tricked each other...
?

ITSUWARIBITO

Volume 13
Shonen Sunday Edition

Story and Art by
YUUKI IINUMA

ITSUWARIBITO ◆ UTSUHO ◆ Vol. 13
by Yuuki IINUMA

Original Japanese edition published by SHOGAKUKAN.
English translation rights in the United States of America and Canada arranged with SHOGAKUKAN.

Translation/John Werry
Touch-up Art & Lettering/Susan Daigle-Leach
Design/Matt Hinrichs
Editor/Gary Leach

Printed in the U.S.A.

Published by VIZ Media, LLC
P.O. Box 77010
San Francisco, CA 94107

10 9 8 7 6 5 4 3 2 1
First printing, December 2014

www.viz.com WWW.SHONENSUNDAY.COM

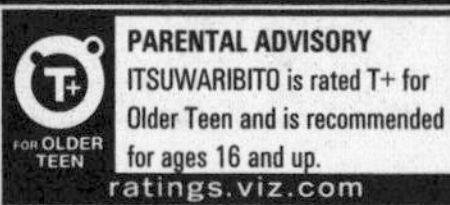

ISN'T GOING OUT FUN, POCHI?

WHAT? AREN'T YOU EMBAR-RASSED DRAGGING AROUND THAT UGLY PIG?

P-PIG ...? BUT POCHI'S A TANUKI!

I WAS TALKING TO THE TANUKI.